Trusting in

God....

*Kristan
Loven Peace
Barbara*

I Am More

Than

I Think I Am

By

Barbara A. Jacobbe

Published by
Inward Reflections, Inc. and
"Inward Reflections" TM ® pending
P. O. Box 1747, Brockton, MA 02302

Reprints of the Paintings
are available through
http://inwardreflections@homestead.com

Available at special discounts for bulk purchases
And sales promotions from the publisher

ISBN 0-9746783-0-9
Library of Congress Number - 2003099237

First Edition

Printed in the United States of America
by

J & R Graphics
155 Webster Street
Hanover, MA 02339
781-871-7577

<u>DEDICATION</u>

I dedicate this book to all the people who believed in me when I did not believe in myself and all of you who called me to become and do more than I ever thought to do.

I also dedicate this book to all of my friends who encouraged me to write this book and who kept on telling me "others need to hear and learn from the process that your writings can teach"!

I dedicate this book to my beloved daughter......Rachel.... who passed away too early to realize her dreams and who now encourages me from heaven.....!!!!

I also dedicate this book to my husband John...... who helped me put this book together.... and so we have learned to be a team!!

I dedicate this book to all of you who may read it and be blessed by it........

I dedicate this book to my GOD who has blessed me and protected me throughout all my life and I know HE will do the same for you.

Barbara A. Jacobbe

THE PAINTINGS IN THIS BOOK

The paintings depicted in this book

are

original paintings done by the author.

These are only a small sample of her paintings.

The author has set up an internet connection

for those who would like to obtain copies of

this artwork or those paintings contained

on the following website:

inwardreflections@homestead.com

If no one had ever shared with me or showed me how
to love and how to believe;
The trust I now have in a loving GOD I would not
h̃ave been able to perceive!

"REFLECTIONS OF LOVE"

I feel compelled by a strong inner force to write this book;

I write it in spite of the fact that I have never written before!

I know the many doubts of insecurity I have felt in my life.

I traveled a difficult journey to discover a GOD I could trust.

So now I share herein my thoughts found in quiet meditation!

If this journal helps one soul to believe in themselves more quickly;

Or prevents one person from hours and days of struggling within;

If this journal speeds one to discover a GOD who loves us greatly;

Then I know that all of this was in accordance with a greater Plan!

I have no education how to present what is called a "proper" book!

All I have is a desire to share love with you that you see a loving GOD!

A GOD who loves me the same as HE does each and every one of us!

My road to discover HIM was difficult – but if we but take a moment...

We will see our beauty as never before in "Reflections of Love"

"From HIM"!!

FOREWORD

*Rainbows bow to your beauty....butterflies envy the ease in which you fly.
You are a free spirited Phoenix.....blazing blue against the darkened sky.
You are a tall flower......defiant of the wind........!!!*
Written by CJ to Barbara

- -

*Phoenix: A bird that rises from the ashes to begin a new cycle of years.
Reborn idealism or hope........a person who has been restored after suffering calamity.*

- -

*Others see the true you and me.....and they can call us to higher levels
than we ever think possible for ourselves.*

*God uses HIS people – you, me, others to love and heal each other into
wholeness. So many of us are fractured by difficult childhoods – tragic
events – and because of it live in pain. We then begin to search and as we
do, many of us question, "Is there a GOD who loves me and wants the
best things for me?"*

*This book is about my own searching, and as I struggled to try to make
sense of all the pain..........That is, if that is possible to make any sense
from it! Pain is an invitation to grow. I have learned..... "Difficulty and
struggles in life are inevitable – Pain is optional"!!*

*As humans we need and want the pain to stop! But, sometimes pain
needs to be experienced and felt.....and then it becomes transformed into
grace so we can learn.*

*As a young child, I was always searching for beauty. I remember living
in the city. Alleys were my playground.....concrete all around me. Then
one day I spotted a tall, blue flower growing along a wall. I was thrilled
and amazed by its beauty...and I wondered, "How did it grow?"*

*Perhaps, it was at this time in life, that I began my search to find
answers to and for the meaning of life! That blue flower was a weed;
but to me, it was the beginning of hope that there was more to life than
just concrete walls.*

*I lived most of my life as a victim. I was always held tight in the grips of
fear. I had no self-esteem! I learned how to survive, but did not learn
how to thrive!!*

(Continued)

As a young child, I remember sobbing when I learned the truth about Santa Claus! I so wanted to believe that HE was real because I needed to know that there was someone who would bless me and love me!!! I realize now, that it was then that I began my search!! Was GOD real or was HE just made up like Santa Claus?

The writings I am sharing are the thoughts and insights I received on my search for the meaning of life. Could a GOD, if real, really love me? Could I find HIM in this world so often bleak? Was GOD bigger than my problems or were my problems even too big for HIM to handle?

The earlier part of my life, I lived as "meek Molly"! Life was to be feared. Then one day, by grace, and while in pain, I dared to believe that GOD was real. I began to look for proof to make HIM real..... and I found HIM!! With HIM, HE promised I could do all things - not fear all things!! With HIM, each challenge in life was an opportunity to grow! I surrendered to the hope in HIS reality and I discovered HIM!!

Through HIS grace I became "assertive Sue" claiming my rights as a beloved child of GOD. HE was always for me, and believed in me and wanted me to grow into all HE had created me to be!!

I hope and pray, as you read this book, you too will discover the GOD I know. HE created you – HE loves you – HE believes in you – and, HE wants the best for you! You are HIS Greatest Miracle.... and ..out of the ashes in your life, you too can rise like the Phoenix. New life is possible for you.

GOD, through the blue weed I so admired as a child was calling me to be a tall flower defiant of the howling wind. GOD calls us in the wind and HE helps us to stand firm. Nothing in life can defeat us when we know we are one in GOD!!

Believe in yourself............GOD does. Trusting in GOD, you are more than you think you are! Then, you too, can rise up against the howling wind to become far more than you ever dared to imagine!!

You are a beloved Child of GOD!!

Barbara Ann Jacobbe

Table of Contents

Table of Contents

Table of Contents

Table of Contents

Pain

Confusion

and

Struggles

The Storms of Life

There are many lessons in life I can learn when I
begin to feel sorry for me!
Then the LORD sends a blind man who has accepted
life so that I can see!

ACCEPTANCE

How I struggle with my life Oh LORD;
I am finding acceptance can be so hard.
I am human and so I struggle against it!
In spite of the fact I know what I must do.

I wish I could leave it in YOUR hands.
Not doing that LORD I find that it hurts;
Acceptance is when I say "Yes O Lord".
To all and everything that life does bring.

Not saying "Yes" is my hardest struggle.
I struggle because I want to feel the hurt.
Yes, maybe I cry a bit so I can find myself;
I might enjoy my self-pity; it can be so easy!

But, alas, LORD, you won't let me do this!
How much YOU must love me not to allow it!
YOUR examples of acceptance are all around.
If only I would take my eyes off myself to see.

I look out the window and I find YOU there!
When I go to Chapel, YOU are with me there!
I see the strength of a blind man going to pray!
His example shows me acceptance in his own way!

He passes by my house each and every day on his way;
Tapping his cane - somehow finding his way to chapel.
He walks to places when I take the car to drive me there;
He is blind Lord, but does more than I do without any help!

He is blind....but his strength he must find and see in YOU.
I want to feel sorry for myself...but then I hear the tap, tap!
When along he comes, never stopping - but on and on he goes!
He is in the rain, as I cry out in amazement... "How can you?!"

He is YOUR example and YOUR presence for me, Lord to learn.
He has heard YOUR good news so he goes on day in and day out!
Thank you Lord for letting me see so now I can learn from him.
He has accepted and lives a full life, he is blind but yet he sees.

It is strange that even in the parade of our life one
person stands out;
Like an old soldier in a parade showing his courage
and lack of doubt!

<u>AN OLD SOLDIER</u>

How everyone loves to watch a big old parade;
The music plays on as the bands go marching by.

The children's eyes light up with anticipated joy
They eat popcorn while balloons are everywhere.

Left, right; Left, right; on and on they march...
In the midst of all of this struts an old soldier!!

He is so proud with his back stretched so erect!
He steps higher than those younger than he is!!

His boots are polished so much they are shining;
While his smile shows he has pride in his country.

It warms my soul to see such pride outwardly shown.
I wonder how many battles that this soldier has seen.

How many struggles has this tough man overcome?
He marches on when others his age can hardly walk.

I know he struggles to strut so much that it must hurt.
I ask, "Would he stop when others less his age will quit?"

No! He would not stop because he has overcome himself;
His age is not a barrier to himself and, more - he lives free.

So march on old soldier each and every day that you want.
For your strength of example will warm the hearts of men.

Forever you will always be an example to others of courage;
You never give up as you keep the beat as the band plays on!

May your smile encourage us all to continue life like you;
Strutting and standing erect like you learning to never quit.

When I see something that is not as
pretty as I want it to be;
I forget about a caterpillar whose beauty
is hidden from me!

A CATERPILLAR

A caterpillar crawls around and around;

Not knowing where to go...or what to do;

It does not seem to know what it should do;

Nor, more importantly, what it will become!

Then one day it becomes ready to transform;

It goes within a very tiny and tight cocoon;

It wraps itself within the dark and it waits;

While nothing appears to change or happen;

Transformation and change has already begun;

The miracle of becoming new still a-waits!!

How many times have I wished I could change?

I would like to crawl and hide inside a cocoon;

Coming out after I become the person I want to be?

Change can be so painful when I do not know what
it will even bring;
Yet GOD knows my hidden beauty when to my old
self I would cling!

<u>CHANGE</u>

I feel so lost since my cocoon, as I know it is gone;
It has broken open and now I lay here wondering!
I no longer know what I thought I knew as my home;
Everything I thought that was secure is changed or gone.

I feel that it was cruelly and quickly taken away from me.
Everything I depended on outside of YOU has disappeared!
Life slips through my fingers as I struggle to hold on fast.
My mother role is over now that my children have grown.

Now what? I remember when my Mom hung onto me...
I felt the resentment within me swelling up inside so large.
I remember my feelings when I wanted to become who I was!
I was not just a daughter; I was more; but I felt she limited me!!

I knew within my soul that I was getting ready to fly loose; and
I felt being pushed back in a dark cocoon and being held down!!
How my mother must have felt like me as I am grieving this loss;
But now I know it is time for me to go beyond into the next phase.

But here I am, I don't know what this phase is or what it brings;
How scary a feeling it is I am entering a new life by leaving the old;
An old life no longer serves me now that I have left my comfort zone!
I need YOU to guide me; yet nothing happens; I must trust YOUR word.

YOU are creating something new like the caterpillar when it changes;
From what it was once....to now being a creation even more beautiful!!
Yet like the caterpillar while it is in the cocoon waiting for the change;
I must be patient.....I must wait....and most important...I must trust!!

*Confusion and fear are feelings which take over the
person and get in the way;
They prevent me from knowing who I am and my
GOD to Whom I must pray!*

CONFUSED

*How confused and puzzled I am about myself and my life;
My spirit feels so drained and I am so hurt by how I feel.
Help me to feel YOUR Love and Power so I am full of YOU;
It seems I am lost when YOU seem so far away once again!!*

*My prayers seem to go unanswered no matter how many times;
I ask over and over as I begin to wonder if YOU hear or care.
I realize by past victories YOU tell me that YOU ARE THERE;
So why am I so weary and feel like I am in a desert that is so dry.*

*I feel that I will not be able to endure this emptiness much more;
Why oh why is YOUR Love and Peace hidden from my inner soul!
I can't find the peace that I once had with YOU not so long ago;
I am lost in this lonely world for I am so dependent on YOU, Lord.*

*I depend on YOU for strength and direction how to cope with life!
Everywhere I turn, the door is closed and I don't know it will open.
YOU said, "Ask and you will receive". Yet nothing seems to come;
"Knock and the door will be opened!" But I cannot find the key!*

*"LORD, my fists are sore and my hands hurt so much from banging!
LORD, the door still won't open when I must find the answer soon".
Somehow I know the solution to what I need has to be inside of me;
I need to look if I have accepted this life as YOU have meant it to be?*

*The hurt I feel within reveals the many negative feelings I must have!
I feel so alone and I am deserted; yet I know that my feeling is untrue!
Maybe, I feel this way because I have deserted YOUR great Love for me.
I let depression and discouragement overwhelm me and forget about YOU!*

*I have stopped trusting anything but can I give it back to YOU once again?
Can I surrender into YOUR love and wisdom again which I do not feel today?
Feelings just are and are not the truth when the truth is YOU are there for me!!
YOU pick me up when I fall and want to help me when the world seems so cruel!*

*Help me see YOUR wisdom in all things and to hold my hand when I am hurt.
I am fearful but when I believe in YOU and know YOU are always my friend;
You will bring me to the living waters where I will be restored to where I can be;
The person YOU intended me to be - without confusion or fear for YOU love me!*

*I sometimes feel that life can be dreary when things
are not going right;
But the lesson for me to see is things change when
dark turns into light!*

DARK TURNS INTO LIGHT

The hush of the morning is pregnant with the change....

The wonder of silence is broken with stirring in the dark...

As the creatures begin to wake the quiet becomes so loud;

The beginning of a wonderful new day has started!

Slowly the dark night turns into a dim haze with life;

The crow calls, creatures run and the birds flutter!

Dawn's light begins to flow through all of nature;

As the sun's rays start to shine...darkness is no more.

A new day is being born and new life has begun again!

It is at this time that I see the precious message it brings;

Things can change like dark turns into light each new day.

Depression is such a lonely place to be in and difficult
for anyone to invade!
It is not because we do not want to draw the shade - but
because we are afraid.

DEPRESSION

How my heart aches deeply for those who are in depression!!
I am crushed with their pain and I want to help them find relief.

I want to reach out to hold them and to touch them with my hands;
My heart is heavy for all of them as I stumble and falter in my efforts!!

I realize that I alone cannot help them in the pain of their depression!
I remember the times that I felt the same abandonment aches as them!

I picture a window shade pulled down so tight on a dark cloudy day;
That no light can come in ... and that is how depression seems to me!!

On a dark cold day, most want to pull the shade up to allow the light....
To enter the room to let in as much light so we can make things bright!

But, depression pulls the shade down so tight especially from within;
So no light is allowed to enter our soul to show us the brightness of life.

LORD, YOU wait for us to pull up the shade so we can see YOUR light.
YOUR sun is always shining bright for us; but sometimes we block it out!

Help those in darkness to want to choose the light and lift up the shade!
Help them to reach for YOUR light and allow YOUR love to fill their void.

11

*When all the elements of the world blow
adversity and it is in your way;
That is the time to let your roots go deeper so
your spirit will not even sway!*

GO DEEPER

*The cold wind blows in the chill of this dreary day'
The wind chimes are crashing against each other!*

*It creates a noisy bong instead of a pleasant melody;
Winter is upon us and I feel the coldness in my soul.*

*I lose the warmth within asking "where has my joy gone?".
I lose sight of my dreams as I am feeling empty and alone.*

*This is the time you call me to go deeper to seek for YOU;
Like the bare tree in winter must go deeper to nourish itself.*

*My days lately…seem so empty…where have I gone astray?
Like the bare tree, I need survive and not depend on outside!*

*Circumstances rule my day just as much as they rule my moods;
They create a noisy clang inside of me where once was a melody!*

*Help me Lord to go deeper for my nourishment like the bare tree;
So once again, I can feel the warmth within me by finding YOU!*

*As fierce winds blow and chills of winter come to enter my soul;
I must go deeper within myself to discover I stand secure in YOU.*

Tiredness is never my friend but always will be my foe!
When I have GOD I have enough energy not to go slow.

I'M TIRED

Why do I feel so tired and very weary today?

Taking a small step is even too much for me!

When I tried to pray and meditate upon YOU,

I found I was so tired I fell asleep so quickly!

How upset I became when I realized this fact;

That this short nap for me was a necessary thing!

Though peace filled me as if I slept in YOUR arms!

I felt guilty needing this sleep because I had asked...

That YOU mold me so I could help those in need!

I had let YOU down because I need to trust you more!

Needing sleep meant that I had let myself be drained!

I often worry about all that I want to try to do for YOU!!

I become drained quickly when I rely on my own energy.

I forgot YOUR promise to fill me if I but trust in YOU.

*When I find myself going the wrong way as I travel
on my way,
It is because I have not read directions or listen to
what YOU say!*

<u>OPPOSITES</u>

I cannot know full…unless I know empty…

I cannot know peace…until I know turmoil…

I cannot know light…until being in the dark!

My good is revealed to me since it is within me!

Often I do not appreciate what I have until I need!

I choose to always stay in the direction of YOU, and..

To see shadows of life as opposite from YOUR Light.

I don't know why I got off the bus or places where I am
very comfortable in life;
It is like I am riding a wild roller coaster where I find
things full of fear and strife.

ROLLER COASTER RIDE

Somehow today I left the bus to get off;
I find myself now riding a roller coaster;
I was comfortable on the bus ride of life;
The ride which was my usual way I lived;
This is because I am just a passenger there;
Where I could just let YOU do all the driving!
I hate roller coasters because they are too fast;
They have sharp curves or steep ups and downs!

I do not feel very safe on my roller coaster ride;
It is not like I felt when I was riding on the bus;
On the bus ride of life, I knew just what to expect;
At least I could fool myself thinking that I knew!
When I was on the bus, I experienced great highs;
Because this was the times I felt I was close to YOU!
Now I am riding a roller coaster and I am full of fear;
I feel I will explode feeling that I am in the pits of despair!

When troubles pull me down and I am looking for the answers;
Solutions evade me because YOU are the one who is in charge;
My fear also holds me back and I do not like this wild, wild ride;
All the security I had before and that I am searching for is gone!
Only in YOU can I find security; so I must search for YOU again;
LORD, let me get back on the bus so I can trust my world once more;
Only YOU know why I am going on this crazy wild roller coaster ride;
LORD, guide me back to where I am comfortable so I can be with YOU!

*If I never knew pain I would never know how
to change;
I would find the feeling of the joy of relief odd and
strange!*

SET FREE

*I experienced an Easter morning for me;
When I was set free from excruciating pain;
I suffered a migraine headache that I can get;
And, no matter what I did, it would not leave!*

*A precious day slipped by that I couldn't enjoy;
I struggled to fight the pain without any relief;
Fortunately when I awoke the next morning;
The headache pain was gone, and I was set free!*

*LORD, may I always have compassion for people;
Especially those who suffer always in constant pain!
A pain that never seems to end no matter what they do;
Must be like being entombed in a prison or a dungeon!*

*May they have YOUR resurrection YOU had on Easter;
And, may they be set free from their pain to find relief;
But, if their pain returns, give to them YOUR Peace;
Consoling them if they may not be set free from pain!*

There is beauty in snow falling on a winter's day if
we just look at it right!
Just like life can be full of struggles or can look at
GOD to make it bright!

<u>SNOW FALLING</u>

I woke this morning to see the snow falling;
I did not appreciate it as a beauty of nature!
I was so caught in the struggles of life I had.

All I could see was the burden of my shoveling;
I thought also of the perils & difficulty to drive;
When did I lose my perception of nature's beauty?

Where did I lose my wonder for fun in fallen snow?
It covers earth and transforms it from drab of brown;
It makes a thousand diamonds sparkle in the sunlight!

Silence covered the earth; YOUR Presence is so strong!
The beauty & splendor of YOUR snow blanket I didn't see;
I looked outside my window seeing only my struggles today!

My attitude colors my day and how I see and look at it to be;
YOUR wonder is always around me, but so often I miss it all;
Often I see struggles when I can see wonder in snow falling!

*Spring is eternal and a lesson for us as we see the
new buds of spring!
But, we need to search within our self to discover
what life can bring!*

<u>SPRING</u>

I feel it's presence in the wind that change is here;

The ground that was so barren is pushing up green!

The tree that was so bare in winter is sprouting buds.

Tiny crocus are in bloom and the robin sings its song;

Around me change occurs as new life is springing forth;

Like spring, new life can stir in me for my spirit to awake;

To believe in the impossible; to reach beyond what I know!

To awaken as buds in spring discover their joy of creation;

I discover as I awaken like spring what YOU created me to be!

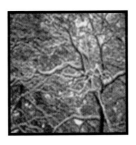

Nature in its bareness trusts in GOD that new life will be coming in the spring;
We must trust that GOD will bring us out of misery and heal us from its sting!

THE BARE TREE OF WINTER

I look out my window and see the tree so bare;
To human eyes it appears dead with no life at all!
But deep within, I know that life is still going on;
Its roots deep in the ground to nourish & sustain it!

No longer is it depending on the warmth of the sun;
Nor on the rain for its roots to drink and to nourish it!
The cold winds blow hard and the ice coat its branches;
How often I look at my day and feel my dreams are dead!

They look like the tree, yet I hear YOUR voice within me;
It encourages me to trust in YOU where I will be supported!
When the winds of adversity blow, then I must always trust;
New life springs forth in me like buds in spring do on the tree!

We have experienced enough springs to know that this is fact;
Life comes forth from the trees & shrubs that appears so dead!
If I place my faith in YOU, I will know the same can be for me;
From my bare tree of despair, new life will stir as I trust in YOU!!

The clam has a very hard shell so it can live safe in the sea and it remains alert;
It is no different when we shut out the world just so we can keep from being hurt!

THE CLAM SHELL

I have been so hurt by many people including friends;
Who have been angry and in their pain lashed out at me!
I see myself as a clam soft and mushy inside a hard shell;
When I open my shell to let love in I take a risk of being hurt!

If I get hurt, I tightly close the shell to protect me from harm;
I dare not open up so I am safe; but then I keep everyone out!
LORD, help me to risk opening up again and not be so afraid;
Let me learn to know safe, healthy boundaries so I can open up!

Help me realize that it is hurting people who hurt other people!!
If I think it is personal, I will live my life with a fully closed shell;
I have to risk opening up and to sometimes peek to see if it is safe
With YOU at my side, I can risk opening up out of my clam shell!.

*A most reassuring time in our life is when we have
a Father's Love!
A blessed gift it is but if we don't get it here it will
come from above!*

THE FATHER'S LOVE

*How I have always yearned for the FATHER'S love;
A Love which is beyond anything that I could known.
When my burdens are heavy, HE wants to carry them.
Imagine yourself trying to carry some heavy packages;
As you move on and you become heavily weighed down...
Impossible for you so you cry out; and your father comes.
He reaches out to you but first picking you up in his arms.
Then he picks up the packages so you can sigh with relief.*

*No matter my status in life, I have a FATHER like that!
HIS SON, my BROTHER, wants to bring me close to HIM.
For HE tells me that HIS FATHER is also my FATHER!!
Many times, I have often wondered if this could be really true.
The FATHER has also created me and made me HIS very OWN!
HE often sees whenever I struggle and HE yearns to help me then.
When my burdens are heavy, HE always wants to carry them for me.
Patiently, HE waits; because he wants me to ask HIM for HIS help.*

*There is nothing that my FATHER cannot or would not do for me.
Nothing is too big in my life nor is it ever too small for HIM to do!
I have a FATHER who loves me as no human father could ever do.
HE knows all of my needs and sees them before I even ask for them.
But, first I have to learn to let go of all of my heavy burdens and then...
I need to call on my FATHER for HIS help and let HIM lift me up high;
When I do ask HIM, HE comes running to help me, and then I will know;
I feel a Father's loving arms hold me as HE comforts me with HIS help.*

*My problems overwhelm me at times and I feel so alone and even fearful.
That's because I struggle to do things myself without any help from HIM.
How foolish I am, when I know my FATHER always waits for me to ask;
HE is waiting for me to call out to HIM to ask for help in my time of need.
I can't–HE can – whenever I let HIM do the work since I can't do it alone.
If I could learn not to be so proud or stubborn and trying to do it by myself.
When I cry out to let HIM lift me up, I am comforted to find HIM so near;
I find myself cradled in the Father's arms of Love; I am safe & all is well!!*

*How is it, when we start to grow up; we forget to see
beauty with childlike eyes?
Yet, if we stop seeing with innocence and curiosity,
something inside of us dies!*

The Wonder Of It All

*As a little child, I could see wonder all around me;
I would marvel so as I watched the fierce wind blow;
So strong and powerful, yet still invisible to my eyes;
Where did it come from and how; I used to wonder?*

*I'd listen to wind chimes with their sounds so healing;
I'd see the wind blowing the trees and stirring the leaves;
The clouds would move and I'd let my imagination see…;
Sheep…castles…mountains…and often an angel or two!*

*I loved to play with bubbles as my magic plastic wand waved;
It turned the liquid into bubbles and I would rejoice with glee;
I'd see a butterfly and slowly I would draw close to its beauty;
So much reverence I had, knowing I dare not touch its wings!*

*Butterflies were meant to be always free and fly so I could wonder;
Now the firefly, that was the best for me on a dark night all lit up;
A bug that could shine was amazing for me to see with my curiosity;
I would collect them in a jar - where did my childhood wonder go?*

*When did I stop seeing? When did I stop wondering and be in awe?
We are all so anxious to grow up - who told us to put wonder away?
Wonder is the ability to see all God has created and to rejoice in it…
In the rush of growing up…we stopped pausing…stopped looking…*

*Time began to push and we focused on pursuits we had to accomplish;
We took simple things of beauty and pushed them aside just to grow up!
Today, I took a moment to pause, because I had a child with me to watch;
The child looked in wonder at all creation - I began to see wonder again!*

*I reclaim the child that still lives in me and now I give her my permission;
To appreciate all the gifts which surround me - like I always did as a child;
Help me Lord to see with eyes of a child and give me a heart of gratitude!
So I will take the time to see all YOUR gifts and give me a heart of wonder.*

*It is easy to lose myself while dealing with my daily
struggles and all of my fears.
Writing things down lets me believe in myself until
YOU can wipe away my tears!*

WRITING SO I CAN BELIEVE

I find that I need to begin to write down all of my thoughts;

Perhaps that is how I will hear YOU speaking to my inner soul!

In my daily struggles, I become too wrapped up in my troubles;

Like I feel today; I am so tired physically and mentally either way;

Does it matter which one? I only know that I am dependent on YOU!

I need YOU to help me from faltering or from getting so tired in my soul;

This only allows the fear to invade what I was once had - a peaceful mind!

Through these trials YOU can reach me to show me the way I need to go;

Help me to learn to give when I want to run – I am only running from me;

YOU want me strong when I protest because I am weak in all my struggles;

YOU want me to be confident in myself when my knees only want to shake!

Help me LORD to believe in myself and to find YOU while writing to believe!

Discovering

Light

In The

Darkness

The Guiding Light

Many times when I go to a chapel simply to meditate and to pray;
I find it difficult to do when I'm tired and have worries of the day!

A Chapel Visit

I went to chapel tonight to spend an hour with you.
A quiet hour of not pleading; but trying to listen!
The first ten minutes were extremely difficult for me;
My thoughts filled being tired and the rush of the day!

So many thoughts and worries filling my mind;
It seemed those first ten minutes were ever so long!
It was because I was being so conscious of only me!
Lord, my thoughts were about me and NOT of YOU!

Thank YOU, Lord for YOUR kind patience with me.
Thank YOU for YOUR great gift of LOVE toward me.
As I slowed down, I began to feel YOUR PRESENCE!!
And my thoughts finally allowed me to be aware of YOU.

Peace came finally; then thanksgiving and awareness;
The other fifty minutes began to fly by ever so quickly.
I experienced such joy and peace in this chapel praying!
I was beginning to feel I was actually living with YOU.

I did not want this hour to end as it went by so quick;
Surely, I thought that heaven must be like it was here....
But even more....if I could only imagine what it holds;
Lord, I love YOU and YOU love ME...My soul overflowed.

But now back once more into to the world I must go.
I don't want to return to its hold as I leave this place;
I desire to remain with YOU....here in this quiet Chapel!
I need YOU to keep me strong in YOUR LOVE and GRACE!

I found YOU here within me in this holy and quiet chapel...
Now I must leave but I can bring YOU with me as I return;
Yes Lord, keep my heart strong until I visit here once more!
Let me feel heaven's kiss while I am still living in this world!

*There is nothing more beautiful than the sun that
lights up the skies;
Sunrise starts a new day with such glory for me to view
with my eyes!*

A SUNRISE

*This one morning I awoke earlier than I usually do;
It seemed so dark and gloomy; and I sat in the silence.
While I looked outside through the darkened window!*

*Then I began to see a flicker of red starting to appear;
The sun spread across the darkened and gloomy sky.
Soon, red filled over what was once dismal and black.*

*It became bright and magical, as I looked out in wonder;
As it changed a sky that had been bleak and dark before!
I was witnessing a miracle of a great new day being born!!*

*Light now filled the sky; which had just been so bleak before;
How much we can learn from nature as it teaches us lessons!
Teaches us so we can enter new beginnings; or make a change;*

*While we wait in the darkness we are confused and bewildered.
Then it appears suddenly out of the darkness we can see the light;
Hope suddenly appears and begins to lift our hearts like the sun;*

*Hope fills us like the sun fills the sky as a new day begins at each sunrise.
How wonderful it would be if we could be like the sun each day of our life;
To start off each day with the miracle of a new beginning like the sunrise.*

*It sometimes gets very difficult when I am weak
and feel alone;
That is never the case because GOD gave me an
angel of my own!*

ANGEL IN MY POCKET

*I have an Angel box I carry in my pocketbook;
To remind me who I am and that I am never alone!
This angel reminds me that I am God's very own.*

*Angels may come to me in many, many forms.
Ministering to me with gifts of love and peace!
He helps me to hold no matter what when weak.*

*God is good and always wants the best for me.
But, sometimes I find life very difficult and hard.
Yet my angel comes to bless me as she stands guard.*

*I hold on to this box when I need to remember;
That GOD is for me and I am safe in HIS Plan!
GOD holds me ever close in the palm of HIS hand!*

*There is no separation between me and my GOD.
For HE holds me close and together we are ONE.
That is why I have my angel and the gift of HIS SON.*

I never knew what power a simple smile could have on
a lonely soul;
Until I gave an old man one of mine and saw his spirit
become whole!

AN OLD MAN'S SONG

LORD, I saw an old man today crumpled up in wheelchair;
He looked so sad and alone, I wanted to reach to touch him!

I wanted him to know that I loved him as I tried to talk to him;
He could speak very little English and spoke broken phrases!

YOU LORD, would not let me stop there – you gave me a smile;
Surprisingly, he smiled back at me and my heart filled with joy!

He started to hum an Italian song and I asked would he sing it for me?
He replied, "Oh no – I sick – No good to sing" I guess he had no hope!

I then said, "Please sing it for me – even if you are sick you can sing"!
"They will always remember your song" and to my amazement he sang.

He sang so loud and clear and he touched me with the beauty of his
song;
When I went to leave, he hung on to me because he didn't want me to go.

I promised him I would be back – and – he will always be a part of me;
He showed me how to let my love be shown without fear or saying a word.

Without any communication, but just a simple smile given to am old man;
I was able to get an old man to open up his heart and let me in with a song!

The love of a child can teach us so much about God's
great Love for me;
It must be just like heaven I am feeling when I bounce
Caleb on my knee!

CALEB

I have been blessed with a special and loving grandson!
I can look at you and see your dad when he was young.

Your dark brown eyes sparkle with wonder and excitement;
And, you can give love so easily with just a look or a smile!!

I was blessed with his love tonight in his look as he said,
"Nana, I love you so much - can I sleep with you tonight"?!

He loves me enough to leave the security of Mom and Dad;
To be with me - he is such a gift as he shows his love for me.

He crawls into bed with his precious stuffed animal – a "duck";
As we lay in the stillness, he whispers to me, "I love you Nana"!

And, I put my arm around him; he feels secure and falls asleep.
I look at his angelic face and I feel what a wondrous moment it is!

The simplicity of a child is a wonder of GOD - a lesson to be learned.
I experienced a glimpse of Amazing Grace and Unconditional Love.

It is easy to stay within the darkness which seems safe for it is how we begin;
But, we were meant to be more and that is why we are called from deep within!

<u>DEEP WITHIN</u>

Deep within my inner being;

Darkness is calling for light!

The light is like a great magnet...

That beckons within calling for me..

To unite every cell and become alive;

And, become all I was created to be!

To come out of the deep dark cavern;

And leave doubts back there deep within!

How sweet it is to see the world with such curious eyes of wonder as my foundation;
Then I need to be like a child again to look around so I can see all of God's creation.

EYES OF WONDER

To have those big eyes of curiosity and wonder!
To be able to see with fascination as a child sees!!

The years rob us of so many of life's little joys,
The joys that are with us and always surround us!

LORD, if I could see like a child just once again;
I would see the sunrise and rainbow in the clouds;

The ant that rushes here and there and all about;
The bird that sings so in melody so sweet in the tree;

Things of beauty and wonder I would no longer miss;
If only I had eyes of wonder so that I might truly see.

*We will search all over the world to find
"Unconditional Love" to give and receive?
But we can find it only from our GOD when
we just search for HIM and believe!*

GOD LOVES US UNCONDITIONALLY

*Most of us have never experienced "Unconditional Love"!
Although we have searched to find this kind of special Love!*

*Often, we see and find unconditional love in an animal we have had;
This pet has given us their total devotion and loves us no matter what!
They crave our full attention as they purr loudly or wag their furry tails;
They always want to be with us and always want to show us their love!!*

*Have you had the benefit of a friendship where when in their presence?
They always try to make you feel you are more than you think you are!
If you have experienced a pet or a friend like this, you have been blessed!
Both are but small examples - a fraction of GOD's unconditional Love!*

*Today, we can desire to know this GOD of unconditional Love intimately!
No longer is the barrier of our youthful teaching of a harsh judging GOD!
Or taught of a GOD who wanted us to always be good & even to be perfect!
This teaching which served to prevent us from ever feeling GOD Loving us.*

*But, today, that teaching is gone so we can become aware to discover;
A GOD who is craving our attention and is anxious about you and me!
HE always wants to be with us and HE wants us all to know HIS Love!
He wants to reassure us that we not forgotten nor are we ever a mistake!*

*Because we are HIS loving creation and we are precious to HIM in HIS eyes!
HE loves us unconditionally and it is each of us HE wants to always bless!!
HE cannot deny HIMSELF ever because we are One in HIM and He in us;
HE is with each one of us, as only HE can be and is "Unconditional Love"!!*

*How often have I told myself that I do not want to
ever grow old!
Then I have to be like a child to behold the world
for it to unfold!*

NEVER TO GROW OLD

To be aware of the moment; is like being able to never grow old!

*Have you ever watched a child, ever curious, discovering the world?
The wonder in their eyes watching clouds flow by; the joy of hearing;
They hear a bird sing and then reach out to touch or feel everything;
They touch soft tiny kittens or the bark on a tree - so much to discover;*

*A child has much wonder and curiosity - where did the child in us go?
Did we get bored with life's wonders by letting our curiosity die in us?
We discovered and than went on…to what...so many of us are bored!
We reach for more and lose sight of all the wonder that is around us!*

*We get pulled down by our burdens and struggles in life and miss out!
We do not even hear the bird that is singing or see a tiny hummingbird!!
We need to take time today to look at our world as through a child's eyes!
By staying open to all the wonder we will hear the birds sing to us again!*

*We can realize they sing just for us as they sing on their perch in melody!
Just as the night sky reveals their stars twinkling bright just for us to see!
The sunset that closes the day with magnificent colors of different hues!
The sunrise blazing red as it welcomes a brand new day for us to begin!*

*All of this just for us; even the small dandelion waiting for us to pick it up!
Bubbles floating in the air and we can watch rainbows magically appear!
We will never grow old; but only if we keep our spirit of wonder alive in us!
If it is difficult, just hold the hand of a child and follow them into wonder.*

I often forget to look for hidden messages during my trials;
If I look beyond what I see, from tears I can makes smiles!

Out of The Junk Pile

In the midst of troubles, it is difficult to believe;
That good is often being worked out for me.
All around me is constant struggle of the day;
And, I am tempted to look at only the problems,
I forget that I can, instead, look for the solutions.
Solutions are hidden from me because I did not look!
I was too wrapped up in the problems that filled my life!

Today.....however, I witnessed a MIRACLE!!!
A SIGN OF HOPE....

OUT in the backyard is what I call my own "Junk Pile";
A pile loaded with broken branches, tree limbs, and leaves!
It is full of PILES OF LEAVES raked in the corner of the yard.
After many years of putting all of this junk in this great big pile;
During a time I was facing turmoil and uncertainty about the future,
I looked out the window and saw a brilliant burst of color in the pile!
JONQUILS, never planted by me, had pushed up through all the JUNK.

HOW my heart and my spirit rejoiced as I heard YOU gently say;
"Never lose hope, my child; I am with you so never, never give up!!!
Out of the confusion, pain, and struggle you are in and you must face;
I AM CREATING SOLUTIONS AND A WONDERFUL, NEW YOU!!
My sign to you is coming out of the JUNK that is going on in your life;
That just like jonquils, something beautiful can and will appear for you!
All you need do is wait; "IF YOU JUST PLACE YOUR TRUST IN ME"!!

*How can I learn from a little seed planted in the
ground to grow?
It has to disappear and die to self before it appears
for all to know!*

PLANTED SEEDS

*When I plant a seed, I know it always holds a promise;
As I dig the ground and I then place the seed gently in...
Faith tells me to always expect the promise it will grow.
I pat the dirt down over the seed and leave it on its own.*

*The seed then slowly begins to grow to reach its glory.
For within itself, it knows that it is more than just a seed!
It also knows that it must wait until it is time for it to bloom,
So I look each day but all I see is what appears to be nothing!*

*I struggle with myself - I want to dig it up to see what is there!
Deep inside I also know if I do this, I will surely kill this seed!
So it is with my seeds of faith to plant them and for me to wait!
It is hard for me to trust when I see what appears to be no hope!*

*When I wait, I must trust that a miracle for me is slowly growing!
Though I see nothing, my "seed of faith" will carry me to victory!
It is not yet the time to see or know what GOD has in store for me;
I wait until my miracle of hope bursts forth like the planted seed!*

*The safety that I seek for myself is not in the world
that I know!
It is only in the LORD where I am safe and so my
soul can grow!*

SAFETY

*Where can I find safety? Can I believe it is ever in this world to find?
How often I am fooled to believe that it is there for me to grab or hold!
I often struggle with all kinds of fear and with the "what ifs" in my life!
What I have is YOUR'S and YOU reassure me that all YOU have is mine!*

*I know if I could just meditate on this daily it would transform my mind!
How I want to be strong, yet I seem to always struggle with all my fears!
Do I trust enough in YOU, when everything in life seems to pull me down?
I struggle to bring myself up, knowing in my heart YOU want the best for me.*

*Why do I not see or feel this truth when I know YOU have great plans for me;
But today, I can only see pieces of the puzzle; & I can do nothing on my own!
I know YOU tell me I don't have to worry because YOU always watch over me.
YOU will guide me through my struggles and fears and lead me to find safety!*

*When we recently moved, both the cats were terrified, crying and meowing;
I put them in the bathroom to keep them safe as we moved all the furniture in.
They didn't know they had come to a better place as I tried to keep them safe;
All they knew was fear even though I was doing all I could to protect them!*

*God brings us into a new place every time we seek HIS help to make us safe;
When fear strikes, He consoles us and we feel secure as our fear disappears!
HIS plan is for our Highest Good as He brings us to a brand new dimension;
He promises us we will never be abandoned by HIM but we need to seek HIM!*

*My anchor is in HIM…as the winds of change blow and I am tossed all about;
I am secure as HE holds me tight in HIS arms & calms the storms around me!
I am entering new dimensions where I am in a better place for me to live anew!
Where I can enjoy all HE has promised me; I am well and have found safety!*

*If you have never found a sand dollar or held one
in your hand
You do not know the joy it brought to discover one
in the sand!*

SAND DOLLARS

*Along the coast we walk with sea water swirling around our legs;
We are seeking a treasure found under the water - a sand dollar!
Our toes become instruments as we poke with them at the bottom.
We discover our treasured dollar and joyfully hold it in our hands!*

*It is perfect and round and my children jump for joy at this find!
We search for more; one is never enough for each want their own.
It was during the summers of old – what memories they hold for us.
Life rushes by swiftly -my children are grown and no longer home.*

*Life can sometimes beat us up; like the waves during a heavy storm;
My son came home, his spirit wounded, & while we walked the beach;
I saw him search for sand dollars but he found only the broken pieces.
Yet the memory of finding them long ago moves him to keep searching!*

*I say to myself, "There is hope; so keep on searching & keep looking";
We keep searching & not get discouraged even finding broken ones;
We can still find what we seek - LORD YOU restore this broken son,
He is seeking healing; he is so broken like the sand dollars he found!*

*The waves of life have worn him down - give him courage to keep looking...
For the beautiful, whole sand dollar that waits for him alone to be found.
Bring back to him the joy he once had as he held a sand dollar in his hand.
The joy that was in his heart summers ago when he found one in the sand!*

41

Do we always hang on to the dead bushes in our life
for as long we can?
Or dig them up to rid them from our life so we can
follow GOD's plan?

THE DEAD BUSH

Last summer I had a beautiful azalea bush so full;
Its blossoms thrived with color until the winter came!

This spring I waited for this azalea bush to blossom;
I waited and waited but no life appeared to resume;

The bush looked stark and bare and seemed to be dead!
All around new life was appearing but not the azalea bush!

I gave up and then I tried to pull it up but roots grew too deep;
How often have I a dead bush in my life that I need to get rid of?

It matters not if it is an old belief or resentment that I hold unto!
When I hold unto them hard and fast, part of my heart has died!

As hard as I try on my own to pull the roots of these false truths;
I am helpless to remove them because they are rooted in me deep.

No life is left to appear in my heart because of how sad I become;
I need to turn to YOU to ask for help - I can't do this on my own!

Even if these roots are deep-I know YOUR Love can release me;
I can get rid of the dead bushes in my life; if I but turn to YOU!

*When we feel we are always rejected and shoved over
to the side;
We need to let our GOD nurture us back and forever
be our guide!*

THE REJECT SHELF

*I found a Calla Lily plant pushed over to the side;
It had overturned – and its leaves were everywhere!
A beautiful white Calla Lily drooping and rejected;
It looked hopeless sitting on the store's reject shelf!*

*Something nudged my heart; I took it home with me;
I tied yarn around it - it stood tall again as it should!
Now it is full of life instead of dying from inattention;
I asked, "LORD do I let myself go like this Calla Lily?*

*I give and give of myself until there is nothing left of me;
Then I feel lonely and discarded as if I am on a reject shelf!
YOU come along and rescue me until I stand firm and tall;
YOU nurture me to reassure me I am more than I think I
am!*

*YOU remind me that to love others I must first love myself;
And fill myself up with Love or I end up on the reject shelf!
If I lose my way YOUR arms surround me to hold me up;
I can blossom with joy, and no longer be on the reject shelf!*

Do I just lose myself in the celebration as we end the
old to begin a new year?
When I fail to see it as a new beginning for me and to
rid myself of all my fear

THE YEAR 2000

The year 2000 and a brand new century have begun;
A new age is here when this New Year is now upon us!
I look out my window and see only the night is very dark;
The magical is here when the clock chimes it is midnight!

It is a very sacred moment when a new millennium begins;
It moves in so quietly but how can we capture the moment?
Was it like this in the beginning as darkness became Light?
I have witnessed and experienced a new beginning of time!

This can be a time of empowerment and thanksgiving for me;
A time for healing and restoration and time to give my praise!
A time of joy and awareness that there are no limits put on us!
That we are only bound by fear & limits we create in our mind!

Your Presence is our gift as we feel YOU come into our hearts!
I can sing with the birds, hear the crow and whistle of a train;
The silence of morning is broken as life stirs all about so new!
YOU end darkness, the old and fears as we begin the year 2000!

When I have eyes to see and ears to hear, why do I
always miss out?
I know it's because my head is down in my sadness
and in my doubt?

TO BE TRULY ALIVE

To be truly alive to life, with so many colors, and its warmth;
And, around me the world full of sound and echoes of wonder;
This was not always the case for me when I had no joy inside!
I had eyes, but could not see; I had ears, but I could not hear!

I walked the earth as if sleeping missing out on all the wonders!
Because I refused to open up my eyes and ears to see or to hear;
Like many who are like the walking dead refuse to look at YOU!
We are too busy living our lives seeking goals we will not achieve!

It was when I began to seek YOU did my eyes and ears open up!
That was when I was at my lowest point and could no longer go on!
I felt nothing was left and it was then I dared to reach out for YOU!
It was by giving up the struggle that I found life and I found YOU!

My eyes began to see colors of the rainbow- my ears heard melodies!
Were they always there when my heart was heavy in pain without joy?
Holding on my pain blocked YOU out 'til I gave YOU my aching heart;
I no longer walk as if I am dead - YOU came to me and I am truly alive!

*I often find myself running blindly helter-skelter
here to there;
Time can be my ally when I slow down seeking
God in prayer!*

<u>TOO BUSY</u>

*At times I am too busy and all I can seem to do is run;
I run in circles using a lot of energy but I go nowhere!
I need YOUR help and guidance to calm me in my day;
I have a thousand things to do but all I fight is the clock!*

*The clock is my enemy but it should be me friend with time!
That is not true when I am fighting YOUR Plan for my day;
I hear YOU whisper to me, "Go slowly amidst the crowd"!
"When you are running; you whiz by me and miss MY help"!*

*I should not be puzzled getting nothing done running in haste;
For I am back to steering the wheel as I take back the control!
That is when I run into total confusion going from here to there;
When all YOU want me to do is ask for help planning for today!*

*LORD, I need help to slowdown, take a breath, one step at a time;
I ask YOU LORD, what is YOUR Plan for me & how to use my day?
Can I take the time to slow me down to make Divine Order my reality?
It is amazing what I can do when I am not too busy & I put YOU first!*

*I get confused about how and where I can see and
touch my GOD's face;
It is simple for me because all I need to do is reach
out to the human race!*

TOUCHING

*How I would love to touch the hand of God; what a joy it would be!
I would search high and low just to have one glimpse of YOUR face!
I would climb the highest of mountains to have the joy of seeing YOU!
I would walk a thousand miles if only I could walk in YOUR Presence!*

*But where can or would I find YOU? Are YOU off in some distant land?
YOU said that wherever we find Love – that YOU always would be there!
If so, have YOU been wearing so many faces or have been in many forms?
When my arms reach out to hug another, are YOU the ONE I really hug?*

*If I am grasping a small child's hand, am I touching the hand of YOU?
The smile I give to friends or strangers, am I smiling at a glimpse of YOU?
The prayer I offer for a homeless person is that prayer said just for YOU?
Then I should realize if I believe YOUR words, where Love is, so are YOU!*

*It should be obvious to me now- YOU are not off in some far distant land!
YOU are in the faces of all the people that YOU send for me to see today!
When I choose to love all these YOU sent to me today - then it is YOU I love!
Whether they are happy or sad - YOU are there - & so I touch YOU in them!*

Letting

Go

Letting Go

Life has so many problems which I try to solve all by myself in vain;
GOD is up anyway – so I can give to HIM my worries and my pain!

A GOD BAG

I have many problems that seem to overwhelm me;
I seek answers, but then the solutions I cannot see;
I struggle and search hard but control I do not find.
Despair clouds my heart, and my vision. and my mind.
Where do I turn to – Whom do I seek – Where do I go?
Am I alone in my journey and do I have a life of woe?

Do I hold on to my problems and just endure the pain?
I can't seem to go on any longer; do I struggle in vain?
Why is my life so difficult that I do not take it in stride?
Do I face my problems or is it that I have too much pride?
I know I have no real solutions and have fallen into despair!!
GOD, are YOU big enough to help me – do YOU really care?

Learning is so difficult – can I turn to HIM and begin to share?
When I become desperate enough and learn to seek GOD in prayer!
I finally must let go to let YOU relieve my pain grown so great!
I know I can't hold on much longer; I need release from my fate.
YOU hold the answers to give solutions to release me from my fears!
YOU are bigger than my problems and YOU can wipe away my tears!

YOU have promised long ago that YOU will always be with me!
All I need to do is allow YOU in and open my heart so I can see.
So often I feel I am in a darkened room where there isn't any light;
Because I have shut it out by drawing the blind and shade so tight!
Even when YOUR sun is trying to shine through with YOUR Love;
I still refuse to lift the shade to let YOU or your sun in from above!

Today, I choose a better way; now I lift both the blind and the shade!
I have found it is easier for YOU to find solutions since I have prayed.
I found the answer I needed that YOU gave me in this pretty velvet bag!
Where now I can place my worries and cares; no longer for me to drag;
By putting them in my GOD bag; these problems too big for me to solve;
I now turn them over to YOU – trusting that today my worries will dissolve.

Now that I can place these problems in my beautiful and velvet GOD bag;
I finally have surrendered – I feel peace – and my spirits no longer sag!
Either I choose that I can believe and receive or I can doubt and go without;
YOU wait so patiently for me to decide to have no more famine or drought!
I want to be ready to let go and let YOU in so I cannot allow my feet to drag!
I am ready, I believe, so I can receive the peace I need by using my GOD bag

53

I fill my cup with so many ideas of my dreams and plans!
I lose sight of YOU and take myself out of YOUR Hands!!

AN EMPTY CUP

Lord, there are many times when I am confused;
I do not know what to do or how or where to go!

I fill my cup with my own dreams and desires;
I leave no room for YOU or YOUR direction!

How often I think I am making such great plans;
And, I work very hard to make them come true.

But nothing - all the doors I knock refuse to open;
I find I am confused....where does the answer lie?

Finally, I stop to listen to the stillness that is within;
There. I find YOU, .and I find where my answers lie!

It is when I am full of my own visions and dreams;
I do not see the better plans YOU have in store for me!

Help me to empty my cup so that YOU can fill it up!!
Not with my desires and plans, but fill it with YOURS.

When I do, my heart sings, now I am in YOUR grace.
Help me to listen to YOU and to follow your direction.

I have emptied my cup now, .so I can hold YOU more;
Fill my empty cup with YOU so that I will know the way!

I ask for answers when they have always been there
in front of my eyes;
That is because I forget the past and I start to believe
in the world's lies!

ANSWERED PRAYERS

Tonight, I reflect on a gift YOU give and forget too often...
That in spite of disappointment, YOU have answered prayers.

Too many times, I find myself pleading for YOUR assistance;
I must find ways to handle life's sorrows when I forget the joys.

I don't thank YOU often enough and too often I ask for help;
How do I know YOU are real? – How do I know YOU even care?

These I ask in spite of receiving a thousand answered prayers...
Where you calm my fears and doubts and reassure me with signs!

YOU help me to overcome what I always thought to be impossible.
YOU are changing me LORD, or perhaps I could say it another way;

That YOU have allowed me to change and to become what I should be;
The person who YOU created and always wanted me to be aware I am!

A person with talents, skills and confidence that comes from YOU to me;
In spite of failures and disappointments you have brought me through!!

I no longer have to fear because together we can handle any situation;
No matter how difficult or impossible it may appear together we will win!

When all appears dark....YOUR love and light sees me through these times;
As long as I don't give up or turn my back or call it quits because of my fear!

Because I know YOU love me and I know YOU are real and will be there;
I see now how often YOU have rescued me from myself and times of trials!

So Lord, I need to try to concentrate on the many answered prayers for me;
And, not ask for things or plead for answers which I know now will be mine!

*Forest fires are deadly and consume every living thing
in their way;
If we concentrate on our trust in GOD, pain in our life
will not stay!*

FOREST FIRES

*Forest fires begin with a tiny spark; the winds blow and feed it.
The fire grows with a roar, and destroys everything in its path!
Loving someone who has a chronic illness is like a forest fire.
It creates within the mind a fear which can consume our peace!*

*We do not know what and when that tiny spark will ignite!
The fear of course, is that this time, that person may leave us.
My security and all that I know will be destroyed in an instant.
I wait helpless; knowing the fire is there and I can do nothing!*

*My fears grow deep within me, as I realize I have lost control;
Then suddenly from the sky rain pours down to drown my fear!
The rain of reality for my forest fire helps me to let go of control;
Control is an illusion - for when we try to control, the less we can!!*

*Help me LORD, to enjoy the forest, the birds, the shade and its peace!
If I trust in YOU, how can I let all my fears focus on the "what ifs"?
Can I stop the ocean from tides?   Can I stop a fire from having flame?
If I can't do these things, where did I get the idea that I had all this power?*

*I wish I did, but I also know it is the illusion and fear of losing one I love!
I also know that from the ashes of a forest fire, new life begins to appear;
Help me to trust in YOU; and help me to enjoy the one I love just for today!
Life is not in my hands, so I surrender to YOU for quality of time to spend!*

It is so difficult for a wife to see the one they love
be sad or struggle or scarred;
It is worse to find they cannot help no matter what
they do and it makes it hard!

HELP HUBBY

LORD - help my husband; he is feeling so low & down;
I want to reach out to love him and help him so much!
But, he has built such a solid barrier around himself;
He sits around and his spirit is so sad and discouraged!

LORD - help my husband; I have tried but it is in vain;
No matter what I seem to do, I cannot seem to help him;
I either say the wrong thing or I say it at the wrong time;
I am suggesting the opposite of what he thinks he needs!!

Letting go is so hard to do; but letting go of him I must;
I find that I need to place him in YOUR hands for care!
I believe that YOU are more powerful than I could ever be!
He is very hurt and the world has beaten him up so much.

YOU never promised us a rose garden in this life on earth;
But, YOU have promised to help us overcome if we but ask;
So many obstacles, struggles and even pain he is dealing with;
I find it so very hard to accept that I cannot fix or help him!!

You call me to stand by and love him even if I cannot fix him;
I surrender him to YOU; trusting YOU to heal him in his state!
In his pain and struggle, may he finally find the answer in YOU!
For when the world defeats us so badly - only YOU can restore us.

*I hold on to things that can control my mind when I
know what to do!
I know I can overcome them if I just let go and turn
them over to YOU!*

HOLDING ON

*Why is it that I cannot seem to let go of things?
I know that each time I hold on to a resentment;
I am held down like Gulliver was by tiny strings!!
A giant taken over by little people while sleeping!!*

*Resentments hold me tight and I forget who I am;
I become obsessed by someone who has hurt me;
I refuse to let go of pain but instead hold it tightly;
What hurts do I endure? - What am I holding onto?*

*The resentment allows someone to enter into my head;
It takes control of my mind with many of my thoughts;
Yet, I am bigger than any of my resentments and worries;
I am small when I let someone "rent space in my head"!*

*LORD, help me to release the hurt and pain from my mind;
For they will slowly poison me and the way I look at this day.
Resentments hurt me, and by holding on, I become a victim!
Turning it over to YOU, I am able to overcome by "Letting Go"!*

*Trying to control things beyond my power is like holding
onto a string ever so tight;
It is the same when I bring pain upon myself because I do
not let GOD make it right!*

<u>LETTING GO</u>

Have you ever wondered about different things?

Am I alone in this big world left to drift all around?

Or, is there a Power greater than I am to guide me?

Is there a power holding me and all the stars in place!?

I have so many concerns and struggle to find solutions.

Concerns weigh me down, robbing my days of all of its joy!

It reminds me when I flew a kite – have you tried flying one?

I struggled to get it off the ground until finally it went up!

I watched it soar higher and higher as my heart soared with it;

It started drifting over the ocean…I reached up to grab the string!

It cut into my hand – and then, I found out what letting go meant!

Holding on was too painful…letting go meant turning over power!

The power that I thought I had but quickly found how painful it was!

Letting go – gives God control – like I did the kite I could not control;

Where I will go is up to a Power greater than me – only by letting go!!

*We often try to treat sorrow in life as if it could squeeze
through a funnel?
We forget to trust in GOD and that there is "light at
the end of the tunnel"!*

LIGHT AT THE END OF THE TUNNEL

*Life is so full of sorrows that it is like we are living in a tunnel!
Can we still trust YOU, when all we see is turmoil and despair?*

*We all make choices every day to travel on one road or another;
One road is with YOU the other is deciding to go without YOU!*

*The road without YOU....is dark...lonely...and full of despair!!
Do we wonder why we feel shattered and alone or without help?*

*The road with YOU...holds hope with solutions we cannot see!!
We believe YOUR promises are true and we live with seeds of faith!*

*We believe what is not yet within our reach will still come to be!
We walk a thin line in a dark world knowing it has YOUR Light!!*

*A Light bright enough to guide our footsteps each step of the way;
We put one foot in front of the other following YOUR beam of Light!*

*It is enough for us to see our way though the future is not so clear;
The only reality for us is this moment – that is where we concentrate!*

*It is our choice to follow the darkness or the small beam of Light!
I choose to walk in the Light knowing darkness will not overtake me!*

*I trust in YOU to show me the way through the struggles I will face!
Pain does not last forever, since I see "Light at the end of the tunnel".*

*A rainbow heart is the gentle heart of GOD calling
to my inner soul;
So I can find GOD's Love in me and discover with
HIM I am whole!*

RAINBOW HEART

*I bought a rainbow metal heart and hold it near;
Tenderly in my hands, moving it back and forth;
I hear musical tones sent by YOU to comfort me!
Comfort me in a way that I will not be afraid again!*

*I wonder - who created this thing of beauty and color?
More importantly, why does it comfort me so much?
I see it as my heart when I am feeling One with You!
YOUR love for me is soothing me by the rainbow heart!*

*I see YOUR bright Light shining about and within me;
Deep inside my soul, I hear your melody of Love playing...
Sending soothing sounds of music that comfort me within!
YOU are telling me that YOU hold all the answers for me.*

*All I have ever sought after is already within my soul;
Often I have looked for YOU and have not found YOU;
Now I know that I was looking from the inside but outward!
Your gentle Voice was calling me to just look within myself;*

*When I did, I finally found that YOU were already there!
YOU said. "Be still and know I am within you - we are one"!
"When we are one, there is no storm which can overwhelm you"!
"Take comfort in ME & always hold on to your rainbow heart"!*

I do not dance as smoothly with my partner when I try
to take away the lead;
We no longer have the rhythm nor can HE find a way
to give me what I need!

THE DANCE

I love to dance and feel free while having fun;
I feel myself and the band's music becoming one.
I yearn to ride the notes as if I were playing a game;
My heart's joy is dancing just like a candle's flame!

While my soul rejoices and my spirit is being free;
YOUR invitation to dance is just for YOU and me!!
This is wonderful; I am feeling safe as I transform;
I fall into YOUR arms - a dancer waiting to perform!!

The music plays as I take over and then I try to lead;
My way is better because I think that is what I need!!
Soon I lose the rhythm and I start to falter, trip and fall;
Why is it that I always act so and think that I know it all?

So often my mind runs ahead of me when I try to race so fast;
Or, it will drag me down when I go and stay in the painful past!
You do not exist in either place; I am blinded and miss my cue;
Denying this and not staying in the present separates me from YOU!

If I truly want to dance with YOU then I must deny myself to hear...
YOUR voice while I surrender my will to YOU so I can stay so near!
And I must trust YOUR steps of guidance along each and every way;
I need to let YOU always lead as I dance in life so I will never stray!

*Clouds of trouble and strife will always come into all
our lives to block out the sun;
But, for us, the sun will always shine if we turn to
HIM and do not hide or run!*

THE SUN ALWAYS SHINES

*The sun always shines and I wonder how that can be?
Especially when we have days filled with clouds & rain!
Clouds cover the sun so often on dark and gloomy days;
Just as we cover up our hearts from GOD's Love for us!*

*We create the clouds when we refuse to listen to our GOD;
He tells us we will pay a price whenever we refuse to Love!
GOD's Love never leaves us even when we create the clouds;
If we do, we may not see the sun or we may not feel the SON!!*

*Skies may appear dark and gloomy - the SON always shines;
Receive HIS peace to know above clouds the sun still shines!
Never give up and never surrender to life's gloom and despair;
If we but turn to GOD our clouds move to feel HIS rays of love!*

*I can't - but YOU can - move my clouds which I have created;
We focus on negatives - blocking out good YOU planned for us!
When we surrender all to YOU, we feel the SON shining through;
We then will know that YOU will always shine for us like the Sun!*

It is so easy to get very comfortable just like wearing an old shoe!
But when we are transplanted we can grow as we change our view!

<u>TRANSPLANTED</u>

We have been moved once again or are we just being transplanted?
In our strange new surroundings we are feeling so lost and confused!
All is different as new roots sprout for us as we are dug up once again!
I was so comfortable there because I wanted to hang on to the old me!

YOU are the Sun of growth and every breath we draw depends on YOU;
YOUR Loving concern and wisdom are with me in this brand new place;
Surely we will grow even stronger if we but allow YOU to be the Gardener!
YOU know where it's best for us to be to grow to the strongest that we can!

Where ever we are or find ourselves is our space to serve others and YOU!
We do not know on what road or place you will take us but we are ever safe!
Because we always know that YOUR Love and Care will forever be with us;
That alone is sufficient for us as you bring us to new roots to grow strength;

We would certainly die relying on our own strength or we were without YOU;
We need YOU to feed us and water our spirits so then YOU can bloom in us!
So with YOUR guiding Light, we can spread YOUR Love to all that YOU send;
We have YOUR peace within; YOU feed our new roots as we are transplanted!

Learning

From

Nature

Nature's
Lessons

*Even on a cold and bleak February morning we can
find some rest!
If we just sit back and let GOD's sun warm us to
relieve our stress!*

A COLD FEBRUARY MORNING

A cold February morning is with me today.

The snow is falling on the roads and ground.

It is covering all of nature in the frigid silence;

Then the sun appears; my world begins to shine....

Its warmth is beginning to be felt from all its rays!

How wonderful I begin to feel deeply within me!

I start to feel good on this cold February morning.

I close my eyes to sit back to feel the sun's rays;

I begin to feel one with God in the beauty of the day!

Divine Energy fills my being by the Light of HIS rays!

It is at times like this, I become aware that we are ONE!!

*We always need some quiet time and a spot to go
for reflection;
Not only do we find peace in it but it is when GOD
gives direction!*

A QUIET SPOT

*I have found yet another spot to find some quiet;
LORD, it is good for me to take time for reflection.
I watch as all of GOD's creation is speaking to me.*

*It is a rainy day and it is pouring heavily outside;
The wind is strong and blows the leaves everywhere!
It seems the leaves are having a merry chase indeed!*

*This dreary day separates areas of dark from the light;
It makes the color of leaves in the trees seem so bright;
In this quiet spot I see YOUR nature so vivid and near!*

*Let me always be aware of the truth it holds for me to see;
Since nowhere else is YOUR glory so boldly held in view;
Nor told as eloquently than in my quiet spot by the window!*

*It tells me YOU are always near to me and ever by my side;
Like nature YOU are powerful and will always be my guide!
But I must look and reflect on YOU in nature in my quiet spot!*

The tiny mustard seed is so very small that in the hand it is very difficult for anyone to perceive;
Yet it becomes a giant tree reflecting a faith which made it grow that it can be difficult to believe!!

A TINY SEED

I can't imagine a tiny seed holds such life within!
I am also amazed of the many promises made to us;
YOUR saying that – "If I have the faith of a tiny seed;
I will be able to move the mountains" overwhelms me!

Can this promise that YOU made to all of us be true?
Is it that easy to do what seemingly is impossible to do?
What are YOU trying to tell me in this promise of mystery?

Is it that my faith has to begin like a tiny seed within me?
And, through YOUR grace and spirit, that will grow!
That is, based on the simple need, that, first I must believe!

The mountains that can be moved by this seed of faith;
Are the mountains of fear – doubt – insecurity!
As I believe – I will reap; whatever I plant – it will grow!!

LORD, YOU teach me that I create my own reality.
All I need to do is to plant this tiny seed of faith and wait;
As I believe, YOUR Love will create miracles in my LIFE!

*I often wonder why the pine tree stands after a storm
but the oak breaks in two;
I have come to realize that it bends and sways but it
gets its strength from YOU!*

A WINDY DAY

*I sit looking out the window as I hear the wind blowing hard;
I feel so secure and safe within the comfort of my home so warm!
A large pine tree is so majestic, tall and strong and tries not to bend;
But, in the fierce force of the wind, it is bending back and forth!!!*

*As the pine sways, its pine needles seem to be dancing up and down!
It does not break for the pine tree has learned to go with the flow;
As it sways back and forth, it reminds me of how often I soon forget;
Forget to go with the flow and how often I struggle against the wind.*

*I fight the strong wind - somehow thinking I am stronger than its force;
Like the tall oak that stays frozen in its position; determined not to bend.
Yet the oak gets broken in two because it forgets how to bend with the wind!
It forgets that the wind is stronger than whatever tries to remain so rigid!!*

*What tree do I imitate in the turbulence of life and forces of disappointment?
Despair.....and failures.....and shortcomings can shake the roots of my being!
We must learn from the pine tree; to go with the flow and bend to GOD'S way.
His ways seem to confuse us like the tree trying to decide which way to turn!*

*Can we trust HIM enough; so that we just go with the force of the wind??
The wind blows fiercely to force us against our will trying to bend us in two.
Can we stand firmly while still yielding at the same time like the pine tree;
Trusting that there is a Higher Order and Plan with roots secure in HIS love??*

*We can bend and sway like the pine as we face our struggles each day of our life;
With roots that go down deep to hold us up and not yielding to circumstances!
We depend on promises as yet unknown to us and beyond what we are yet to see;
We have a GOD who is an awesome GOD who loves us and HE will never fail us!*

*No matter what the circumstances are in our life and beyond what we can see;
Can we believe with all of our being and trust - are our roots so deep and strong?
Is our faith solid enough so we sway and bend relying on HIM against the wind?
Or, are we like the oak tree too rigid in the way we think that things ought to be?*

*Do we try to force to make solutions but struggle to stay strong against all the odds?
Do we have roots strong in our own power which break in two and fall like the oak!
We have so many lessons to learn from the pine tree who knows how to bend and flow!
It has strength by not fighting against the odds, but trusting it will survive with YOU!*

When a cold winter morning blows fiercely all around making a fuss;
We can warm ourselves with the rays of the sun and YOU inside of us!

<u>A WINTER MORNING</u>

How you always bless me with abundance.

This morning the sun is shining brightly;

While I am lying on the couch meditating!

And the sun is shining its rays on my face;

I can hear the cold wintry wind howling!

Wind chimes are playing wonderful tunes;

While they are dancing in the strong winds!

All nature is astir from the wild chilly wind:

Yet I have my comfort and I am warm inside;

I feel YOUR Light warming all of me within;

Like the sun warms me on a winter morning!

Birds are so tiny and fragile things, but from them I can learn;
A valuable lesson in life that joy is now and not in what I yearn!

BIRDS

In the early morning, just before the sun even shines;
I hear the birds in the trees singing their lovely song!
Greeting the day in melody of musical wonder as a sign;
That no matter what the weather is - it is never wrong.

They sing whether the sun is shining or not at its best;
I always thought that whenever the rain would pour;
That the birds would stay in the protection of their nest;
Yet, they enjoy the rain, flying up and down as they soar.

Perhaps they know a secret that too often we forget;
That joy does not depend on the circumstances outside!
Their joy comes from within and weather is never a threat;
Celebrating here and now and taking the weather in stride.

LORD, may I always learn from the birds you send my way;
That my joy is in the moment no matter what it may bring.
And no matter how difficult the moment is I will never sway;
For I find my joy comes from YOU and like the birds I sing.

*I am so often rushed and crushed by life's busy
schedule of the day;
Then GOD sends a small sign and message just
for me along my way!*

<u>CHICKADEE</u>

*Fall is here and the leaves fall swiftly like the snow.
On and on they fall ever so gently like snow flakes.*

*They blow with the breeze here, there and everywhere;
I sit silently watching all of nature's beauty and wonder.*

*Then suddenly, I feel a soft touch of something on my hand.
A small little chickadee surprisingly has landed on my palm.*

*I hold my breath and look as he seems to hold his breath as well;
We are overwhelmed as we acknowledge each other's presence!*

*This is truly a beautiful gift from GOD and such a holy moment!
And just as quickly as it happened – with a flutter, he flies away.*

*I sit in wonder and awe of how such a small little creature of GOD;
Can stir such unimaginable feelings of wonder deep within my soul!*

*Thank YOU, LORD, for blessing me with such a gift of this as a sign;
YOU brought me ever so close to a tender, little one of YOUR creations.*

*For a moment, I became one with nature in spite of being rushed;
When normally I have no time for me, a little chickadee honored me.*

Sometimes life gives me things I cannot bear and I
want to rave and rant;
Yet, GOD sends me examples of HIS power like in this
dead tomato plant!

DEAD TOMATO PLANT

Today, I rejoiced...as I received a simple and unexpected gift...
I ate a tomato from a plant which had grown in my garden!

Who would have thought that this tomato would have ripened?
The plant had practically died; its leaves were no longer green!

It had such a purplish hue, bent over, downcast, nearly dead!!
I almost threw this tomato plant away thinking it would not live!!

And, yet, faith made me plant this tomato plant in my hope anyway;
For some reason something inside gave me the faith of "letting go"!

I knew I could not control anything in this life and certainly not life;
I thank YOU Lord for letting me trust this way as I gave it back to you!

Even when I didn't believe that it could be when it came to this small plant;
Yet I saw it with my eyes and experienced resurrection as it came back to life!

That tired looking plant sprouted tall, strong and firm again from the ground!
Up, up it grew denying all odds, fate, reason, and beyond what I could believe;

I am grateful that YOU gave me faith and I chose to plant it in spite of doubts;
Despite its appearance of death, somehow I still believed that YOU could give it life!

Help us Lord to always have this kind of faith to trust in YOUR power to restore;
Especially, when circumstances make it all appear hopeless and beyond our belief!

YOU promise with every cross in life that there is a resurrection in store for us;
Our confidence must be in YOU and not trust in just appearances before our eyes!

No matter how hopeless a situation may appear to be to us if we but give it to YOU;
YOU are there with us, and, just as the tomato plant, we will also rise tall and strong!

Sometimes I do not realize how precious just a day for
me to live can be;
The hibiscus plant is a lesson to teach how precious a
day is so I can see!

HIBISCUS

The hibiscus is such a beautiful flower with colors so bright;
Red and orange and yellow hues ever so lovely in the light!!

I watch the bud and it seems to take so long as I wait and wait;
Finally it blossoms and I am so awed by its beauty – it is great!

Then to my amazement – it droops and then right before my eyes;
The blossom lasts only a day – how can this be that it suddenly dies?

All this time to grow and blossom and in twenty-four hours it is gone;
It seems like such a waste; to live only a day not to see the next dawn!

It makes me begin to think, "How important is a day to me and you"?
Like the hibiscus, if I have only a day, I must value it more than I do!

LORD – teach me today is precious and beautiful & made just for me;
Help me to live to treasure each moment of this day for that is the key!

Moment to moment – this day is more than I realize & I need to know;
Tomorrow is a dream – today – NOW is my only reality & chance to grow.

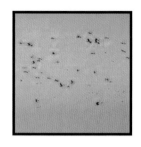

*There is nothing so beautiful in the morning that you
can hear;
As the sound of birds waking you up singing their song
of cheer!*

IN THE MORNING

As I awake...I hear the birds singing in the air!

The melodious sound calls gently for me to wake!

I hear the song of so many singing joy of a new day.

They sing back and forth bringing delight and cheer;

I am so grateful I could sit in the sound of their song!

I know they sing daily, but often don't take time to listen;

Thank you LORD, for this gift today YOU sent my way;

On this still morning, YOU allowed me to hear their song.

*Hearing the sounds of nature all around me doesn't
take very much skill;
But to hear God speaking to me in the silence requires
me to be very still!*

IN THE SILENCE

I try to sit still in the morning;

Seeking YOU in my quiet time!

I listen for YOU to speak to me;

As I slowly breathe in and out!

From silence within me and outside;

I begin to hear the birds singing to me!

It is a whole chorus of sound and melody!

The silence becomes full from the trees in back;

I heard YOUR voice through the song of birds!

In the silence, is my time to just listen for YOU!

*Many times, what prevents having joy and a new way
of life is me,
The reason is I hold onto the past and never let it die
so I can be free!*

<u>NEW LIFE</u>

A large birch tree appears to have died in my front yard.

Its big white branches have fallen right onto the ground.

When I go to remove the tree, I see a tiny shoot trying to grow!

From this decay, is life still within this mass of wood so dead?

I decide to leave the tree alone in case new life is still possible!

I saw a chance for new life to grow – and begin again it did!

From an old tree that died, a new tree has sprung new roots!

It is reaching for the sky, and its leaves are celebrating life.

The old must pass away so that a new life can begin to grow!

LORD, help me to learn from this tree to leave the past to die!

Letting go of what doesn't work; new life can sprout forth in me!

PINE TREES

I sat in the forest of trees and looked all around me;

I saw that the pine trees were clustered close together;

They were like a family – being of all shapes and sizes;

Giant pines, to smaller and smaller, down to a tiny shoot!

All gathered together, but different height, yet all the same!

I see the human family all together, different yet all the same!

While the pine trees seek out the sun and water for it to grow;

We seek to be closer and closer to YOU so we can reach Higher!

So together we stand, some taller than others, some in between;

Some young – others ending; like the pine tree we are the same!

*I never knew before what the rainbows after storms
meant to me as a sign;
It means that YOUR miracles and Light of future
hope will be mine!*

<u>RAINBOW</u>

A rainbow is so very beautiful in the sky;

It is a sign of everlasting love and hope;

They are so full of many beautiful colors;

I often wonder, "Where do they come from"?

Why do they appear only after the rain storm?

Is it the sign after the struggle…after the pain;

That is when YOUR Light breaks through the sky?

It bursts forth in such amazing splendor of color!

I find YOUR Light of Love and Hope shines in me;

Filling me with Love and Hope with YOUR rainbow!

*Sometimes I try to protect myself away from the
world where I dwell;
Then I shut myself in and everyone out trying
to be safe in my shell!*

SHELLS

*How beautiful shells are lying there on the beach;
When we look, we can always find special treasures!
A shell which is so beautiful but hard on the outside;
It held inside something which was soft and delicate!
This shell was the protection for the life it held within.
A life that was so fragile it needed the shell to survive!*

*A shell can also be a safe place for us to hide ourself!
We use it to protect ourself from life's harsh realities.
But, this shell that we use to protect and keep us so safe;
Can also become like a prison to us which keeps us inside!
Not only does it protect us from outside but also from within.
It keeps anything that is good from going out or coming in!*

*It is good to have protection since it keeps us safe from harm.
It also helps to learn what boundaries I need to have and keep;
This is how I know when and where I am safe and free from pain.
The pain which teaches me how, when and where I need to be secure!
But, it is in protecting myself from this pain that leads me to run away;
I also stop learning from life's lessons and receiving YOUR abundance.*

*So I can learn from the pain or I can choose to shut myself in a shell;
Instead of living life, I wrap myself more tightly, cut off from the world;
LORD, I need YOUR help to know when to open up or to protect myself!
I know that I am safe when I am in my shell; but it also keeps YOU away;
I realize that I need YOU more close to me to receive all YOU have for me!
This means that I must learn how to dare to open up and let YOU in for me.*

*To open up I risk getting hurt sometimes, but I also know if I dare not risk;
I will be a prisoner of and to myself locked up forever in my own thoughts!
I will never dare to search outside myself for answers or to find friendship;
But, if I open wide to YOU, YOU can enter to teach me a better way to live;
To learn that I do not have to be in a shell to be safe in my own little world;
I do not have to protect myself so securely that I am a prisoner in my shell!*

*We often wonder what it would be like if we could
reach the heavens so far!
Yet, GOD has made this possible for us to see with a
fish shaped like a star.*

STARFISH

*LORD, YOU have created a wonder-filled world;
When I look all around me, I can see YOUR work.
I see the stars – the seas – the birds – and the trees!*

*I look out into the night skies and see all its beauty;
I marvel at the light from the galaxies and the stars;
Yet I can neither touch nor can I hold these creations.*

*Wonder of wonders, when I look in the sands of the sea;
There I will find a fish that is shaped in the form of a star!
In my curiosity, I can gently hold this starfish in my hand!*

*Only YOU could create such a wonder of beauty for me!!
A starfish – so beautiful – so unique – and yet so fragile;
Now I hold it in my hands; this is one of GOD's wonders.*

*LORD, you constantly remind me through your creation;
YOU have such a wonderful and miraculous Love for me!
YOU reveal it to me often if I only let my eyes and heart see!*

*LORD, you surround me with your wonders everywhere I go;
If I only take the time to look, I will discover YOUR presence;
When I doubt YOUR Love, I will not be able to reach for stars!*

*But, when I find myself gently holding this fragile starfish of the sea;
I realize now, YOU have shown me the way to reach and hold a star!
The starfish teaches me whenever I need; YOU find a way to bless me!!*

*Who would think a simple sunflower could teach what
I need to know?
That it stands tall and firm in beauty because it depends
on YOU to grow!*

SUNFLOWER

*Like the sunflower does – I am searching for YOU!
With every movement of the sun, I am clinging to YOU!
I awake in the morning, and my thoughts are of YOU!
As the hours move on during the day I must follow YOU,
In the confusion of life, I constantly need to turn to YOU
Comfort from rays of Love that I receive come from YOU!*

*When I follow YOU just like the sunflower follows the sun;
I too must reach upward to the sky and I am able to grow!
Like the sunflower grows on its stem so strong and so tall!
Because it always reaches out and yearns for the warm sun!
As YOU fill me with Love I am nourished as if by YOUR sun!
YOUR Love gives me life as the sunflower receives from the sun.*

*May I grow and learn from watching the sunflower grow!
It grows to become so tall and beautiful and ever so glorious.
It is constantly ever reaching up and ever yearning for YOU.
YOU give it YOUR Love and Strength through rays of the sun.
YOUR gift of Love & miracles are the sun of life for me to grow!
I must continue to be like the sunflower and forever follow YOU!*

*If I had to imagine what image GOD would take I
think all would agree;
That He would be like the Power of the Wind - the
GOD we cannot see!*

THE POWER OF THE WIND

*It is a cloudy morning very early in the fall;
The wind gently blowing through the chimes!
I hear joyful, playful sounds of musical notes.*

*Leaves are stirred up by the power of the wind;
As they are laying ever quietly upon the ground!
Now the wind is swirling them around in the air.*

*The leaves blow around in circles here and there;
As the clouds move swiftly across the windy sky;
The power of the wind is blowing them both around.*

*I see glimpses of the sun that fades behind the clouds;
And the clouds keep on marching swiftly by in the sky;
The effect of the busy wind fascinates me by what it does!*

*It is busy and full of force but I cannot see it with my eyes;
I see what it does but I cannot see its strong invisible energy!
The wind reminds me that it must be like the Power of GOD!*

*HE is all Energy – and all Wonder – and an all Powerful GOD!
I feel GOD's Presence in me but I cannot see HIM with my eyes!
HIS energy fills me, but HE is unseen like the Power of the Wind!*

Storms may come our way to overwhelm our spirit or get us down with fears.
But, when we see the rainbow, relief is in store for us to wipe away our tears!

THE RAINBOW

Only after the storm does the rainbow appear – Oh how can this be?
It does not appear on the sunny days which we are always glad to see!
But, only after the dark and stormy days we feel will never stop or end;
The rainbow does appear with its warm and bright colors that it sends!

Why do storms rage before the rainbow sends its colors across the sky?
It is just after the darkness when GOD shines HIS Light of relief on us!
Where once darkness and despair and fear were giving us tears to shed;
GOD allows the colors of Light and Love to fill us to let us move ahead.

Reminding us no matter if we are weak – HIS miracles will fill our heart;
HE will send the rainbow to tell us that with HIM our fears will depart!
They are replaced with HIS Light as HIS brilliant colors jump and dance;
Only HE could bring the beauty out of darkness with Love in HIS glance!

HIS Love turns clouds of fear to colors showing HIS truth for us to know;
HIS Light is what transforms our lives and makes our heart shine and glow!
Do not fear because miracles are hidden from us which GOD wants to give;
HIS rainbows of Light will appear with colors of relief so that we may live!

A bird gives God its glory with the many beautiful,
melodious songs it sings;
We give our glory to GOD by putting faith in HIM
and the peace HE brings!

THE SONG OF A BIRD

How my heart rejoices hearing the song of a bird;
The lovely notes coming from such a small creature!

The birds flutter their small wings from here to there;
Even during time of winter, we can still hear them sing!

Their melody brings cheer to such dreary and cloudy days;
They sing their songs giving faith and peace to everyone!

It's amazing these birds never stop singing no matter what;
If we could only sing no matter how our spirits let us feel!

YOU enable us to sing & smile when the world lets us down;
We are lifted up when covered with YOUR wings of security!

Winds may blow problems in our life but YOU give us a limb;
So we can hang on – and if freezing we find warmth in YOU!

As birds sing glory to GOD, our smiles give the glory to YOU!
YOU give hope to protect us – so we have the song of a bird too!

The fierce wind blows so strong it blows against
everything with force;
But, as long as I stay rooted in YOU I will always
stay on my course!

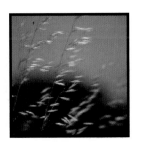

THE WIND

The wind howls as it is blowing so fiercely with such force;

All is quiet around me and then it suddenly comes so strong!

Energy that we cannot see is always around us everywhere;

So when the winds blow, I am aware of its force and strength!

Thank you, O LORD, for giving me such strong roots so deep;

Roots which are grounded with branches reaching out to YOU!

I am being held down firmly because I am always secure in YOU;

Fierce winds can blow, but I am strong because of my faith in YOU!

I Create

My Reality

By What

I Focus On

Focusing

Barbara Ann

*An "empty box" and the gift of today are things for
me to decide how to fill;
GOD has made it this way for HE will never give
us what is against our will!*

AN EMPTY BOX

*I hold a beautiful box in my hand – I wonder what it holds;
I open it and it is empty and I laugh – I expected it to be full!
I wonder about this box for only an "empty box" can receive;
"Today" is the gift YOU give to me – for it can be empty or full!*

*I create my day by the choices I make – "What do I choose today"?
Do I fill it with joy or despair – or my gratitude – or my complaining?
Do I fill it with my hope or dread or in the promises YOU made to me?
I can choose love or fear – the choice really depends on me to make!*

*I hear so often how YOU want to give us our heart's desire and joy;
Yet why do I find so often my box is filled with doubt and despair?
I know deep within, when I finally let go, I can empty this box of mine;
Fill it with what YOU want to bless me with – I must concentrate on this!*

*It is what and where I place my thinking that becomes my reality today;
My reality is what I believe for me and it becomes this that I will receive!
If I believe in lack then I have nothing; if to fight then I have to struggle;
Struggle and fight for what I want because it is what I believe surrounds me.*

*If I believe I am un-loveable, I will draw only unloving people into my life;
If I believe I am a failure, I will never dare to dream in what I can become;
Help me Lord to believe in YOU and to believe that YOU want the best for me;
No matter what circumstances surround me, I am more than what they seem!*

*Help me to open up to YOU so I can realize what I believe is what fills my box;
YOU want to fill me up – can I empty myself of all thoughts of fear and doubt?
YOU can fill me up with YOUR Love and Promises so I can fill my empty box!
Believe and receive – doubt and go without – full or empty – the choice is mine.*

When we blow up a balloon by filling it with air we
make it grow and grow;
Where I focus my attention is the same –
it fills my day with joy or woe!

<u>ENERGY</u>

It is amazing to me how my day changes;
Just from the simple things I choose to do;
My day depends on what I pay attention to;
Where I place my focus decides what it brings!

If I feel rushed – I focus on not having time
To get everything done that I am planning to do;
I become frustrated and I start moving faster;
My day is rushed and I am always on the run!

I get less and less done when I try to race time.
Rushing time gets out of proportion and triggers
Energy that is like a balloon that starts out small;
Then it gets full of air to become bigger and bigger!

What I focus my energy on acts just like the balloon.
Focusing too much on just one thing makes it grow.
The balloon reminds me that this simple fact is true;
Where I place my energy or focus is how my day goes!

When I am rushed, I can change how I am focused;
From not having enough time to that of doing it well;
To do what I need to do and whatever I can do today;
Race against time or do my best - the choice is mine!

The more I focus on the positive and the reality of things;
These are what I will claim for me to have so I can rejoice;
I create my day by how I think or where I place my energy;
Energy can break a balloon or make a day - it is my choice!

*Sickness and struggles often make us see things
in a different way!
Often it is how we focus on things that can make
or break our day!*

FOCUS

*A sinus infection has me in its grips like a vice.
I awake in pain and look for help and advice.*

*I want some relief and I want to get it very fast.
It hurts more to me because I don't want it to last.*

*In the silence of the morning pain grows by the hour;
Help me LORD to focus in on YOUR healing power.*

*I know focusing on pain is what I must always fight.
Instead I need to focus on YOU & YOUR healing light.*

*Then the pain can lessen; that's how powerful the mind.
Creating and building on how I focus is what I will find.*

*When I focus on pain, fear and doubt, those feelings grow.
For like the seed, I reap only what I plant and what I sow!!*

*So what seed do I plant now is what I need to always question;
Help me to focus on YOUR healing power to end my depression.*

*Sinus problems will be replaced by gratitude which surrounds me.
If I focus on YOU, YOUR gifts of healing will come to set me free.*

*Many times I get lost in life and my focus is off and
goals are out of sight;
GOD is there to love and guide me as long as I search
for HIS beacon light!*

I AM THE LIGHT OF THE WORLD

*What a promise YOU have given us - I wonder if it could be true?
YOU tell us that YOU are the "Light of the World" for everyone to see!
And, YOU say, "Whoever follows YOU will never walk in the darkness,
But, they will always have YOU to lead them and find their way home;
YOU are the "Light of Life" to forever guide them so they will be safe!*

*The lighthouse stands tall upon the rock; its light reaches far and wide.
YOU are the lighthouse, shining YOUR light to guide us on our journey!
The night grows so dark that we are tossed to and fro by waves of confusion;
We travel blindly; and often we do not know which way to go or where to turn!
Through this storm of confusion, we see a "Beacon of Light", showing the way!!*

*In my sea of life, I can see YOU in the midst of my confusion as my "Light"!
I know that as long as I focus on YOUR Light, I will find my way safely home.
So often the storms of the difficulties and trials of life pull me down as I travel;
It is only when I look beyond what I can see and search for YOUR beacon of Light
That I will see it is YOUR Light that guides me to find solutions leading the way to safety!*

*Today, I am no longer afraid to travel the unknown or to be caught in the storm;
I know that YOU will always guide me and give me YOUR Light to show the way!
It is when I seek YOU and follow YOUR Light that I discover there is no darkness!
No matter how grim or dim it appears, if I but concentrate on YOUR guiding Light;
The closer I draw near to YOU, the Light grows brighter to bring me safely home!!*

*The darkness can never ground or overcome us, because YOUR "Promise" is true!
When we seek YOUR Light YOU will always be there to guide us to show the way!
And, just as YOU are the "Lighthouse Beacon" – bringing us home to YOUR safety;
YOU ask us to be like the Lighthouse to show others who are frightened and lost;
That they too can travel the waves of life in safety as long as they seek the "Light"!!*

There are many choices I can make in this life!
Peace from within or the world and all its strife!

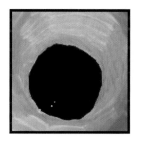

<u>INSIDE OUT</u>

As I meditate this morning in a very quiet spot;

I find the peace so I can go deep within myself!

Fear and doubt I have left behind on the outside;

I find instead, inside of me; light, peace, and safety!

I make a choice each and every day how I will live it;

Inside out means that I see the truth from within me;

While many outer circumstances try to control my life!

In these circumstances I experience what I do not need;

Fear, doubt, and insecurity are what are found outside!

Inside, where I am with YOU; then all is well and I am safe!

Where I choose to live, is up to me! Do I live inside or out?

I falter so many times because I am full of concern
and doubt;
Instead if I search for truths about myself I can end
the drought!

MY STRENGTH

Today Lord… I overcame myself,
For only with YOU could I do this!
Many times my feet have faltered;
And, I wanted to give up in despair!

I believe so much in affirmations;
Speaking positives until it happens!
Despite how I am feeling in the day;
I keep on chanting them over and over;

"The Lord is my strength" and also;
"There is nothing I shall have to fear"!
The power of YOUR Word took over;
And, finally I just felt your peace within!

Turmoil whirled all around outside me;
But, somehow I knew it could not win;
I just kept on calling out to YOU for help;
Until - YOUR peace became my strength!

My day depends on whatever choices I make or
what I plan to bring!
Either I make it cold like winter or I can make
it new like spring!

NEW BEGINNINGS

Spring is now upon us once again!
And, new life again is springing forth.
It comes from the ground of winter;
Where all had once appeared frozen…
New life and hope is bursting through!

Each day can be active in your heart;
It is a new beginning just like spring!
Yesterday is gone; today is brand new!
You too can experience a new beginning!
By your thinking and where your focus is!

Whatever you focus on becomes your reality!
So do I focus on the losses of life or victory?
Or do I focus on the pain, struggles or strain?
Do I focus on what I have or what I have lost?
Do I focus on what ifs or what wonder awaits me?

Do I focus on the rain or do I forget the rainbow?
Do I focus on the love I have or on unknown fears?
We all make our choices each and every day in life!
We create our reality by our thinking and thoughts;
Today is a brand new day; springing forth creation!

So what kind of day will I choose for me or make it be?
An egg is an egg…we cannot change it whatever we do!
Today is today…we cannot change what will happen in it!
You are the only one who will make what your day becomes!
Good or bad – so create a day full of wonderful possibilities!

*In every life there are many pebbles to trip on as we
travel through the day!
But by keeping our focus on our GUIDE we find safety
along the way!*

PEBBLES ON THE BEACH

*Have you ever walked on the beach barefoot?
How refreshing the waves are and how peaceful!
We become a child set free to wander on the beach!
One foot in front of the other we splash along the way.
How simple life would be if we just walk along the sea!*

*But, if we run, we take a chance of tripping and falling;
Yet, if we put one foot in front of the other, we feel secure!
As I walked, I came across many rocks & stones in my path;
They were too numerous to count and panic set in my mind;
I looked at it all at once and could see no way to cross safely!*

*I'll hurt my feet…I'll stub my toe…but then I heard YOUR voice;
I heard YOU say, "One step at a time - you can cross and not be hurt!
Do not look ahead or behind or adjust your eyes to this way and that!
Keep your eyes focused, trust in ME and I will guide you on the way!"
Slowly I ventured; and surprisingly I made it through without a bruise!*

*What a lesson I learned that day - to walk slowly - live slowly - in focus!
I breathed as if it were new life and I put one foot in front of the other!
Staying in the moment, not looking ahead or back, trusting I would be safe!
I kept my focus on YOU and didn't look forward to see all the rocks ahead;
I did not fear the pebbles as I stayed focused moving just as I was guided to!*

*YOUR Will, Love and Peace help to guide me; make my way safe to go on;
You have promised me a way when there appears to be no way for me to go!
But, when I can stay in the moment, and put one foot in front of the other;
And if I keep my focus on YOU to bring me to the path safe for me to travel;
That is how I can walk safely through the pebbles on the beach of my life!*

*I can either see a building close or far, tall or short,
big or small;
It is also my perspective on my life if I see a path or
I see a wall!*

<u>PERSPECTIVE</u>

LORD, I need to transform my mind so I may see the way YOU do!

My outlook on life is so distorted by the way I perceive many things;

I have been a victim so long I view life as one who has been tricked;

I have learned to live and survive one unfortunate event after another!

But now I want things to change for me – now I want to thrive & win!

Where is my focus? I have learned what I focus on becomes my reality.

If I focus on my lack, need or fear, that is what I will always have to see!

If I focus on YOUR abundance and I trust that I can have it; it is mine;

So I live life with new perspective – I have Heaven not hell – it is up to me!

*When life rages around us to upset the plans we have
made take it as a sign;
When there is a snow storm we can just deal with it
and things will be fine.*

SNOW STORM

*I awaken to see an unexpected and heavy snow storm;
The wind is blowing so and I have so many places to go!
I look out of the window and begin to worry as I wonder;
What is going to happen and what is this day going to hold?*

*I create my reality by how I think; am I limited by the snow?
Do I sit and do I complain about this interruption to my plans?
Or are YOU telling me to go a different way on this snowy day?
Today can be a day to rest or do things I never have time to do!*

*What choice can I make and would I do it if I just had the time?
Read or listen to music – paint a picture – or take a bubble bath?
The storm is just on the outside – it does not have to be within me.
The choice is mine – I will not let a snow storm ruin a day for me.*

*Of the many choices I have to make each and every
day of my life;
Do I see the stars or do I see scars – or see the joy or
see the strife?*

<u>STARS OR SCARS</u>

*As I sit in meditation, I realize how tired and drained I feel;
Where has my joy gone and how did my excitement disappear?
My body and spirit and emotions feel so heavy and so alone!
When did this happen, and more important how did it occur?
And then, I realized that I have been just dwelling on my scars!*

*We all deal with the disappointments and many hurts in our life.
Some are so painful to remember that they stop me in my tracks!
Slowly I recall anew and allow myself to go down the road of scars.
I then remember all of the hurts that have been done to me in my life.
Surely to be on this road can only lead me to despair and heartache;*

*But even worse, it leads me to separate myself from YOU and others!
I have allowed myself to forget how to seek, look & reach for the stars.
I have lost sight of the wonders of YOUR creation and the good times;
I blocked out the times you have used my brokenness to guide another;
To lead broken persons to see YOUR Loving Light back to finding YOU!*

*Oh, I miss the feeling of having the joy of being in the presence of YOU;
I have lost the expectation of seeing the beginning of a brand new day;
And, seeing the joy of having friends and family that love and honor me!
I need to look at the joy of knowing that YOU are always with and for me!
I have had the joy of many answered prayers and knowing I am not alone!*

*And, I have the joy of knowing that YOU are in me to bring me YOUR peace.
I know I create my day by my choices and by the many things where I focus;
While I am grateful for what my scars have taught me, they are not me today!
I am what I am because of YOU, & the lessons of the scars brought me there:
Now the lessons are over, & I must go on with life and leave them behind me!*

Today I choose NOT SCARS of life, but I focus on the STARS of victory.

We have jars on the shelf that we fill just like we can
fill our mind with strife;
When we fill it with junk then our beauty and worth
we will never find in life!

THE JAR ON THE SHELF

I have a jar just sitting up on the shelf;
It can hold whatever I want to put in it!
If it is empty, its purpose to be is wasted.
I choose what goes in for it to hold inside.
It can either hold beauty or it can hold junk!

Empty jars remind me of my mind to be filled!
Usually my mind is never empty of any thoughts.
But, so often I fill my mind full of useless clutter;
I change this only when I turn to think of GOD!
Then I fill my mind with good thoughts of HIM!

GOD tells me that I am HIS very precious creation;
And, that I am beautiful in HIS eyes and HIS mind!
He tells me to fill my mind (jar) with thoughts of HIM.
To know who I truly am can only come from HIS Love;
I am a precious child HE created so beloved and whole!

I become what I fill my mind (jar) by what I think about!
If worry fills my jar, then I become a person full of worry.
If abundance fills my jar, I am blessed with so much more!
My jar either holds promises for me or I can have despair;
I need to be careful how I think and whatever I put in my jar!

LORD, help me to fill my jar with gratitude and abundance!
And, any day, if I should forget to place good things in my jar;
Let me quickly empty it out and replace its contents with YOU;
I am filled with abundance so I change my focus and my reality!
Then I fill my jar (mind) with YOUR promises for me that await!

I Can

Dream

Again

Dreams

How many of us have ever watched a goldfish swim
around in his little bowl?
Yet many times we do the same – just swim around
and never reach our goal!

GOLDFISH

Have you noticed the goldfish swims in the same small, limited circle?
Day in and day out – around and around the circle it goes all the time!
I watch it and I wonder to myself, "do you, little fish, ever get bored?"
Because, all you ever see and all you know is what is in your fishbowl.

You live the same thing all the time – over and over each day and night.
Then one day, as a change you are moved into a much bigger aquarium.
In amazement, I watch, because you continue swimming in small circles.
Why is it that you don't realize that you are now in a bigger environment?

Now that your world has become bigger, you can have more than before!
What a silly little fish you are to just continue to swim around from habit.
Then, I realize, that in my world I often act from habit like the goldfish.
I limit myself too often because I get used to my own little comfort zone.

Boring as I make my life out to be, I do the same thing each and every day;
By limiting myself and limiting my circle I never seem to reach for more!!
And if and when more shows up, am I really ready to grasp it or to enjoy it?
GOD, do I realize that you want to bless me with more and more of YOU?

Yet, I find myself holding myself back, and bound by my own little fishbowl;
I keep on asking myself questions like, "What if" or "Is it too good to be true".
And when I do, I am limiting myself and I continue to swim in my small circle!
What makes me limit myself like this, when YOU want to give me so much more?

Do I live in my own aquarium, by keeping my thinking limited and so small?
Like the goldfish, do I take so many days before finding my world has grown?
Why does the goldfish take so long to learn its swimming circle grows and grows,
Before learning to swim back and forth with more freedom than it has ever known?

Help me LORD, to learn quicker than the goldfish by being open to YOU more.
Let me learn that YOU want to bless me and keep my thinking from being small.
I know that in my comfort zone, I may feel safe, but it traps me in my small bowl;
When you want me to live with freedom and abundance in YOUR large aquarium!

So, now do I dare to venture out of my little circle where I live and limit myself;
While YOU patiently wait for me to decide whether to swim small or wide and free?
YOU want me to accept your gift of abundance that you freely give and want for me!!
The question is, "DO I DARE?" – "Am I like the goldfish, or do I want more to see?"

*Have you seen a rose hide its beauty - its petals closed
down so tight;
You may be like the rose when you shut people out by
taking flight?*

THE ROSE

*I love the rose and what it means; and I feel it is part of me;
Tightly closed it is ready to unfold its beauty for others to see!
It leans towards the Light so it can feel the warmth of the sun;
That encourages it to open up – for us to see its total beauty done!
The stems reach deep down to drink water – which makes it grow!
Slowly the rose unfolds as it opens its blossoms for beauty to show.
Its fragrance is being slowly emitted until it begins to fill the room;
Showing the world it has reached its peak and is now in full bloom!*

*We are like the rose – hiding our beauty – because we are so unsure;
We are tightly closed – protecting ourselves – until we feel more secure!
We hold our beauty within us – hidden from others – waiting to bloom;
We are so insecure – we wait to unfold our beauty – as if still in the womb!
When we turn toward GOD's Light, we can feel HIS Love and HIS Grace;
So we can feel loved – so secure and safe – then we unfold to others to face!
Then we dare be like the rose and open up a little and a little more each time;
Our stems reach deeply to drink HIS pure water giving us courage to climb!*

*Water which gives us power, and might, and courage from our GOD on high;
Otherwise, we would be like a rose closing its petals, only shriveling up to die!
Still, you will notice that on each rose stem that there are many sharp thorns;
These are many boundaries to protect it (us) from outside sources as it warns!
These thorns serve as protective barriers only and are not meant to cut or chafe;
They are not meant to give pain to any who approach but are just to keep us safe!
Once we accept ourselves as we really are we can then be like the rose to blossom;
So that we can love ourselves as GOD's creation and see ourselves as awesome!*

*We also can love others as GOD meant it for us to do and as it always should be;
Each smile and each kindness we do for another is just so that we can finally see;
That these kindnesses we do are like the fragrance of the rose who we are within!
The fragrance which comes from the tightly closed bud – finally opened to begin;
To fill each day with our fragrance so unique; and there is no other rose like you;
We need to be unique by ourself and open up – it does not matter what else we do;
We will then go beyond our wildest dreams and become what we were meant to be!
So let your fragrance reach & bless everyone – be still and know your Rose is HE!*

I can never realize my beauty unless I break through
the ground!
The tulip must break the bulb and grow for its flower
to be found!

THE TULIP

There is a Divine Moment when the Spirit lights all my being telling me who I am!
I am like the tulip bulb waiting in the ground to burst out of my bulb so I can grow;
Like the tulip, I begin to stir and yearn for more; so that I am not limited by the bulb;
Not knowing where or how we will do it, we want to reach beyond any limits to grow!

Developing slowly, the tulip reaches a new dimension as it breaks through ground;
At last, the tulip has a new reality so the sun can shine on it as it is at last fulfilled!
It has blossomed at last in its beauty and it grows as it reaches the warmth of sun:
But, suddenly it finds the sun is gone as cold winds fall and the snows fall upon it!

It is covered in the dark once more – this time knowing how to wait for sun again!
In the ground, it will grow again to appear and so patiently the tulip waits for sun!
When it feels warm again as the sun melts its snowy cover the tulip starts to rejoice!
For what was lost has been found once more as it once again moves toward the Light!

The tulip loves brightness more than darkness and tries always to grow toward Light;
It becomes more than it once was as it is nourished by Light, it develops a pretty bud!
So full of joy and being fed by the Light it bursts forth not being able to be contained!
In ecstasy, it becomes what it was always meant to be – a tulip and so opens its flower!

Deep within me lies the bulb seed of who I am; as I draw to the Light I begin to grow!
The journey of the tulip is my journey & I must reach for the Light and all its warmth;
The warmth of GOD for me is so I believe I am more than I ever dreamed or realized.
My GOD has given me the same beauty as the tulip which blossoms for the world to see!

How often have I had dreams for myself but don't believe I am worth the shot?
Why can't I take two dreams and plant the seed instead of just asking why not?

TWO PACKAGES OF SEEDS

I have two packages of seeds and both of them are promised to grow!
One will bring pretty butterflies and the other are seeds from Australia!

Both these seeds are promised to thrive in my area and its environment;
These seeds hold out much possibility if I only have the faith to plant them!

My dreams are like these tiny seeds holding promise as long as I have faith!
Do I dare believe in my dreams and will I plant them in the soil of my heart?

We all have much potential in us that cannot grow unless seeds are planted;
Planted in the faith deep within us; the faith in the Power of GOD to fulfill!

Begin by breaking through the shell of fear which has always held us back!
We then must plant the seed of faith and believe our dreams will come true!

We must always water these dreams constantly by believing in our potential!
Pick a wish or two from two packages of dreams but believe it will come true!

We all have a dream to get something back for
what we lost or we want to do;
It will happen if we but trust in GOD – for HE
wants us to have the best too!

VACATION

I have finally returned to the seashore I love once again;
I rejoice in my heart because it took seven years to return;
A long time to carry the memory of the ocean's glory for me;
I had wondered for a long time if I would ever make it back!

I hoped, waited, & trusted and finally I was looking at the sea;
I see the ocean after seven years; I never gave up on my dream!
I firmly plant my feet in the sand as I let the waves flow over me!
Thank YOU, LORD, for the victory of this moment which is mine!

I run along the shore; I am letting the wind blow through my hair!
I hear the seagull cry the song I love to sing – "I am free once again"!
YOU promise me sun after the rain – YOU promise victory after pain;
We seem to wonder when it will be; but, YOUR time is never our time!

So all we can ever do is stand firmly in the truth of all YOUR Promises;
Then one day we suddenly see it with our eyes as Promises are fulfilled!
YOU never fail us because YOU always keep YOUR Word for us to see;
When we believe in YOU; in YOUR time we will receive – our vacation!

The ocean spans as far as the eye can see – its horizons never bend!
So too are the possibilities for me to grow – for they never end!

THE VAST OCEAN

So much clutter is always in my busy mind;
When I sit down and I try hard to meditate;
My mind swirls busy with so many thoughts;
Idle chatter trying to distract me from my goal!

I breathe so deeply trying very hard to let go,
Thoughts come back; and on and on it goes!
I finally feel YOUR Love fill me with Light...
As YOU break through all of these distractions.

It is the same thing when we see the sunshine;
As it is breaking through the clouds in the sky;
Rays come shining down reflecting bright Light;
Light that seems to leap across vast ocean spans.

I am able to see how far the Light really reaches;
This vision reaches out as far as my eyes can see!
The only limits are what I believe there are for me;
I am free to see and free to be like the vast ocean!!

*Windmills use the force of the wind to create a power
filled with so much might;
While we use the energy of GOD to guide us during
our lives to do what it right!*

THE WINDMILL

*The wind blows and I feel its power – the power of the wind on my face;
I feel its energy without seeing it for it cannot be contained in one place!
There are so many things in my life I cannot know, understand or even see;
When so much power and so much energy and so much Love encircles me!*

*The Energy of God, HIS Spirit & HIS Love for me give me so much Power!
Though I cannot see YOU with my eyes – YOUR gifts of Love let me flower!!
I think back when I was a child and I loved the windmill watching it as a girl;
I thought I could catch it as it went around fast blown by the wind in a whirl!*

*Like the wind YOUR Divine Power is always with me and is always around me;
No more could I catch your Power than I could the fierce wind since it is free!
YOU are my friend and YOU Love me each day and want me to grow ever so tall;
If I don't rely on YOU, it is like I am fighting the wind's power and so I will fall!*

*A wind as fierce as a hurricane can destroy everything that it faces along its way;
YOUR Power I cannot see but it so great that I should get on my knees and pray!
That I will be like the windmill and go toward the direction of power so I will flow;
Flow with YOUR help and energy so I will know what YOU want me to do to grow!*

*YOU always want me to succeed and YOU will always help me to do my best;
As long as I am doing what I can, YOU do the rest so I need not worry to be blessed;
YOUR energy – that I cannot see like the wind – lifts me higher so YOU can embrace...
My every effort and spirit with YOUR great winds of Power so I will feel YOUR grace!*

Inward

Reflections

Friends

On

Our

Journey

Friends

So many times we do not stop to think how we
can help others in need;
To make things "bear" able in life for them just
takes doing a good deed!

BEAR-ABLE

Many of us feel lost and so very much alone;
Times are tough and winds of adversity blow;
The truth really is we are not but yet we groan!
Why is it that circumstances of life blind us so?

Love one another as I have loved you is our call;
This call for us to do for others we need to hear!
Once we know and experience God's Love for all;
Loving one another makes life easier for us to bear!

To hug those who feel un-loveable and are all alone;
To lift those who are despondent and have fallen down;
Reassure those who isolate and may have never known,
Love of others who can dry their tears before they drown.

To "bear" one another's burdens to get them on their feet;
Then we can let God's love living in us help to lift their stress!
This is why He needs our heart, hands & feet for all we meet;
So they can see HIM through us reaching out for HIM to bless.

HE can calm and help those heavily burdened get a new start;
Just by your smile and your hug and your hands all reaching out;
To lift another from pain with your humor and your listening heart;
Your encouragement and your love can help rid them of their doubt.

You are in God's Plan to help HIM reach out to others through you;
Every time you dare step out to help lift another in their time of trial.
The un "bear" able then becomes for them so much more "bear"-able;
Because we reached out to them to reduce their pain or let them smile!!

How many times have I let people's opinion control me
and to hold me down?
But GOD has sent me my special "Earth Angel" so I
can now wear a crown!

<u>EARTH ANGEL</u>

You have called me to be more than I think I am or thought I could ever be;
Life and people have beat me down and told me I would always be less than;
I lost myself in people's opinions of me and so I became lost and confused;
I heard GOD was Love yet I felt un-loveable for I had never felt loved before.

I am a stranger upon this land because no one knew or understood who I was;
In my pain, I cried out and to my amazement, YOU sent me an "earth angel"!
This person knew my pain and told me of the same struggles they had overcome;
This person had heard my cry and having heard me; I finally was no longer alone!

You became a GOD with skin – ONE who could love me and even hug me close;
YOU gave me Beauty for ashes because this "earth angel" believed in me enough;
Soon, I began to believe in myself and I dared believe I am a child of the Most High!
Finally I am loved because YOU had created me to know love and become love itself!

Today, I wear a scarf to remind me of my call to answer those who need my love;
I have been commissioned to be an "earth angel" just like the one YOU sent to me!
To go to the lost and confused to tell them I had been lost and felt just like them;
Because of my "earth angel" I have been found and I have been restored in YOU!

GOD wanted me to tell of HIS love to be HIS "earth angel" reaching out to love;
My scarf reminds me of HIS unfolding Love – it is our covenant GOD and I know;
GOD takes you out of your deepest pain and converts it from ashes to HIS glory!
Your heart was wounded and GOD has healed your pain – HE calls you do the same.

.

This now is your ministry and this is your calling and this is your gift to bring to all;
So go forth and become an "earth angel" – GOD now has skin and it is you my friend;
You are more than you dared to believe you could be and HIS covenant is with you;
You are in HIM, and HE is in you, and you are both ONE; go forth "earth angel"!

*Friends are such a precious gift and so rare it is if
many are given to us;
But if we are always a good friend to them in return
it is even more a plus!*

FRIENDS

*Your glory all around this vast universe, I can't help but see;
The stars and flowers – all wonders that YOU created for me!
It reveals your power and wondrous ways, and how it all began.
Love starts with angels but friends you gave as part of YOUR plan.*

*The angels that surround me are those I can neither hug or kiss;
But beyond all my dreams, these treasures bring me so much bliss!
It is through these angels, YOU have hand picked friends just for me;
Friendships form when I return their love in kind so that I will see...*

*In this journey here on earth that YOU have called for me to live;
The friends YOU have blessed me with are so very willing to forgive!
Their light of love shines brightly and deeply touching my inner soul;
Reminding me I am never alone or far from YOU and that is their goal.*

*Angels in disguise – what better gift can I have than friends in my life;
Who love and encourage me especially during difficult times of strife.
And, when I am confused or lonely, they reach out and hold me fast;
Soul sisters on this journey to help me – so together we will always last.*

*YOU have filled my life with so many wonderful gifts of love to see;
But – the ones I treasure most are the friends you have given to me!
In YOUR great wisdom and love, YOU have given me the very best.
Because of these angel friends in my life, I feel that I am truly blessed.*

Angels normally do not have shape or form we can see or hear;
But GOD sends friends to us in our life so that HE is always near!

<u>GOD'S ANGELS FOR ME</u>

I am surrounded by special angels YOU have sent to me;
Angels who normally cannot be seen or hugged by anyone;
But YOU have given them shape in a form called a friend.

GOD, YOU have blessed me with many miracles and gifts;
But, the ones I treasure the very most are these so precious;
They are the special friends in my life YOU have given me!

In YOUR great wisdom and in YOUR great Love for me;
YOU gave these special gifts of friends just for me to have;
I could feel YOUR love by being wanted by the best in them.

Now I know what it feels like to be so close to YOU above;
For these Angels were once with YOU and now sent to me;
They are friends YOU gave to me so I can feel YOUR Love!

*Being in the presence of one who is sick and dying
is not easy for anyone to see;
We pray it will be swift and peaceful, but we also try
not to let go, you will agree!*

HEART BURNING WITH LOVE

*My aching heart is burning with the love of YOU within;
I prayed with a very dear friend close to going home to YOU!
I felt YOUR presence with us so strong and loving, but yet...
We humans convince ourselves that we are in control of life!!*

*But the two of us knew that this was nothing but an illusion;
That there is so much of life we can neither know or understand!
We can look at the night sky to know that there is so much more!
We see stars shine but do not know where their light begins to start!*

*Millions of stars and they are much more than we can comprehend!
Still we think we are in control – understanding life – oh what folly!!
But when we are in the presence of one who is ill and dying we learn;
All the barriers are down – we speak heart to heart – it is a holy moment!*

*This is the time to glimpse the unknown and where GOD is in control!
I was born on the feast of the Sacred Heart; I felt my heart was burning!
I felt YOUR Love burning between the hearts of both me and my friend;
Holy, Holy, LORD almighty, it was a Love too great for us to comprehend!*

*Yet, we knew that this Love of YOURS was the only thing that was real!
Our eyes cannot see the wonders YOU have waiting for those YOU Love;
My friend knows that she will be with YOU soon in YOUR loving arms;
She will be one of YOUR shining stars and will be finally safe with YOU!*

A very powerful gift that is free and so easy for us to give away;
Is a smile that changes the face of others and makes their day!

SMILES

I find it interesting that smiles are one thing we can give away;
And a smile is something that expresses things we want to say!
A smile brings warmth and fills the human heart with our love!
All without saying a word a smile brings us peace like the dove!

How often I take smiles for granted without giving them a thought;
Yet, they are the sunshine that is in our souls that is always sought!
In all of God's creation, only we can give smiles so big they gleam;
They are a special gift – the soul within us speaking words we mean!

They say the eyes are the windows of the soul within us to give away;
By smiling we show the love we give so others can begin to live today.
This smile of ours can open up our hearts so we give to one another;
The Love of GOD showing us kinship with GOD as sister and brother!

The smile lights up the many dark roads many of us travel in our life;
The smile unites us soul to soul and gives each of us relief in our strife!
Strangers will know a smile when they see it coming their way from you;
GOD gave each of us smiles to give to open their hearts to something new!

Without words, our smiles let us communicate to others who we really are;
GOD loves us as Children of the Light so we can shine like the bright star!
To bless the road of life with your smiles for everyone in work or in stores;
And, if you see someone so sad and without a smile, give them one of yours!

Thoughts

On

Christmas

Christmas

*A simple thing like caroling started when we sang
songs to a friend who was ill!
We sang each year and we found we brought joy
to others giving them a thrill.*

<u>CAROLING</u>

*It is that time of year again when we go Christmas caroling;
We organize ourselves as we get ready to bring joy to others!*

*Our intent is to bring happiness and hopefully peace to them;
They are the ones who are just too sick or cannot go out to sing!*

*When we visit the hospital, joy and cheer fills the air as we sing;
We are a mixture of voices but happiness and joy still fills the air!*

*Many of us cannot carry a tune no matter how hard we try to sing;
By a miracle we sing together and YOUR grace blends our voices well!*

*This year became very special to me and my heart was filled with joy;
A man who heard us singing found peace hearing us sing our songs!*

*Then he asked if he could join our group as we went along down the hall;
He moved his wheelchair and joined in song as we continued on our way!*

*God, YOU show us life's lessons so many ways by sending us YOUR angels;
Who teach and lift us from our burdens when we allow YOU to show the way!*

*Through that man we learned that when we lighten someone else's burdens;
We receive YOUR blessings, and even if troubled our burden becomes light!*

*In the rush of time we can forget that we have a gift
in each and every day;
It is an opportunity to share our love with another person in a different way!*

CHRISTMAS IS EVERY DAY

*Another season of Christmas time is near - here so quick;
The year flies by so fast, that it makes time a thing to fear;
Seasons run into another so that they seem to be together;
But, one thing for sure, Christmas is not just once a year.*

*Every day we can reach out to help and touch each other.
This is what GOD taught us that HIS love is for us to hold!
The world knows more of reaching out for material things;
And, possessions are precious if we can touch it or it is gold.*

*They think of the many presents to buy or they will receive;
It is so empty when one must consider what we take or give.
The objects which are hard and tangible to show our love!
When what really makes another happy is seeing how we live.*

*Too bad that we cannot consider that each day is a special gift;
An opportunity for us to find a way to give of ourselves is a start;
And they are for us as numerous as the lights on the biggest tree;
We live Christmas daily each time we give to share from our heart.*

*Then Christ is born again in our being and in the being of others.
HE lives again only through us and walks in our midst every day;
We can take the time and opportunity to give love instead of presents;
Every day for us is a gift and a way for us to help others not to stray.*

*We need to know that it is fact that we can live each Christmas daily;
When we share our love with each other we get away from all the fuss.
Christ is born again and HE lives by the way we show love here and now;
May Christmas be every day so GOD can live again inside each of us!*

*Christmas is such a special day and should be for
each of us a special sign;
It is not once a year but is a symbol of love we have
to share so HE can shine!*

CHRISTMAS IS NOT ONCE A YEAR

*Does giving gifts at Christmas make this day just once a year?
It is not just for those trying to bring light out of the darkness!
Christmas is a new beginning for every one each and every day;
Because we know the Christ child and HIS love is in our midst!*

*The greatest gifts we have and can give to one another are free,
Are those which cannot be wrapped nor be put under the tree!!
They are gifts from the heart: Love, Peace, Comfort, Care, Joy;
Also the concern we have to give a helping hand at a time of need!*

*How does one put these under a tree or know how to wrap them?
Yet, these are presents we have and what Christmas is all about!!
Each and every one of us is the gift of light shining in the darkness!
We are all the gift of Christmas when the world still seeks Christ!!*

*Many have missed the meaning of the simple way HE was born;
Like many others, they seek someone in a high position of glory!
But many of us still find HIM in the simple stable of their heart!!
They no longer roam the darkness seeking HIM who is not there!!*

*For when we have experienced HIS love and are forever changed!
There is no darkness and light burns from the candle of our hearts.
We shine for all to see like the star shone for those in Bethlehem;
Candles showing the way to others that Christmas is not once a year.*

*My heart is like the inn which Jesus sought on
Christmas day;
If I am too busy with self then there is no room for
HIM to stay!*

ROOM IN OUR INN?

*Do we have any room for anyone else in our inn today?
Christmas is coming again and is upon us once more!!*

*Busy days...where we find ourself hurrying and scurrying;
We go here and there as we finish up our lists and chores.*

*We are caught up with our shopping in the hassle of doing;
We are so busy; weariness is just two small steps behind us!*

*Yet, it is Love which keeps us moving as we prepare to give;
We have no thoughts of receiving thanks or gift for what we do!*

*We open ourselves more and move close to touch one another;
We realize that Christmas is daily when we open up to our GOD.*

*YOU come alive within us deep within our hearts when we do this;
We remember that the inns were too full the day Christ was born.*

*We have to remind ourselves to make room for HIM on each day;
It doesn't matter if our stable is humble to us; HE will always stay!!*

*Opening our hearts, HE makes stables shine with HIS heavenly Light,
Seeing this, others receive love at our inn - for we made room for HIM.*

*Many times my mind is so busy with things that I can
get myself in a mess.
Like untying tangled Christmas lights gets me so upset
and adds to my stress!*

TANGLED CHRISTMAS LIGHTS

*The season of Christmas is approaching us so fast;
The rush of preparing is as if the season will not last!*

*I search and then I find the lights for the tree in a mess;
I discover their being tangled up just adds to all my stress!*

*I plug them in and they all work but it seems like a crime;
The patience & persistence to untangle them just takes time!*

*My emotions are so many times much like these tangled lights;
Just like the lights, I work, yet worry keeps me awake at night!*

*When I meditate, YOU calm me and untangle all my emotions!
I need not let my feelings rule me or cause so many commotions!*

*To finally get everything untangled so I can remain not uptight!
I need to turn to YOU to not get tangled up like Christmas lights.*

Grieving -

I Am

Never

Alone

In Loving Memory

Rachel (Jacobbe) Hurvitz
In Loving Memory
June 21, 1965 - February 23, 2001

Live for the Moment

Live for the moment – live for today.
Before you know it – it's gone away.
Take the time to enjoy each day.
Yesterday is gone – tomorrow yet to be;
Today will never be again – can't you see!

Each day is precious – our gift to behold.
It is worth much more than silver or gold.
Don't waste your time on needless worry.
Slow down – don't be in such a hurry.
Take the time to look around.
And see all there is to be found.

Live life to its fullest extent.
You won't be wondering where the time went.
You'll know that each day was well spent.
Live for the moment – learn to be free.
For in each day we hold the key
To our happiness, joy, and serenity.

By **Rachel Hurvitz**

*Nothing breaks our heart more than losing a child
and the pain of grief always shows;
It shows itself within and so to receive comfort we
must seek it from GOD who knows!*

LOSING A CHILD

*My heart reaches out to your heart - there are no words to express the agony...
Of losing a child - no matter how much they have suffered - our child has gone!
Once we had her or him – now we have a hole raw in our hearts - a broken heart!
Our heart - that by the Grace of God - somehow goes on - it beats now with pain.
As a mother, when we were in labor; we pushed in pain and give birth to our child!
We held dreams and visions for them in our heart, never thinking that they will die!
But they died before their time; as we silently watch them suffer so much before us!
We want to ease their pain; and as our hearts ache, we stand by so hurt and helpless!
We know there is nothing we can do; but love them through all they must endure.
How helpless we are, as we become like Mary who stood before the infamous cross.
While she had to watch her Son, Jesus, die a tortuous death; how cruel was her pain?
We understand the agony she must have felt as we too watch a precious one pass on!
When Rachel died - my heart broke open in such raw pain - I cried and I screamed!
Cried as much as I did as if I were giving birth to her again; but instead in my pain;
I released her to a new life - a life with God - a life for her without suffering or pain!
A life promised to us all who believe in Jesus' promise - that there is life after death!
There we live on, as He did in the Resurrection; but instead with a life full of glory!
A piece of my heart was ripped out; and now a space where my daughter once held...
Will forever be empty - as it should be - for no one can ever fill that place now void!
In the beginning, it was so raw; but slowly God's Grace is now healing my heart;
Reassuring me that my daughter is always with me everyday that I live on earth;
Love knows no separation - death cannot end love - love transforms us all to heal;
We enter a new dimension with our child - we will always hear them whispering;
Whispering in our hearts that faith will bring you into a new inner peace forever!
Telling us life never ends...but is transformed and Jesus will massage your heart!
HE will hold you close to HIS Heart...as HE does our children gone before us;
A piece of our heart is now in Heaven...we will never be complete until the day...
We are together again - which to us is like a cruel fate because we are left on earth;
But, we need to realize that this is not that we live in defeat...but to know beyond...
Any doubt we may have; our children have found their God and they had to leave!
Lord...in my anguish...I have to let Rachel go and allow my child the joy of Heaven!
In my pain of letting go; I will find peace someday though my heart has been broken;
I find it also has been opened; even more tenderheartedly than before, for all I meet;
Grief has given my heart compassion for all I meet from this pain of losing a child.*

Strange what little thing fills the broken heart with the
message that it sends;
An "empty stocking" can have special meaning to the
broken heart it mends!

AN EMPTY STOCKING

As I prepare for Christmas this year I am sad,
My heart breaking with tears thinking of you –
My beloved daughter who is no longer here!

I feel your presence within my broken heart;
But I can longer hold you or hug you near;
Out of nowhere – an idea – I knew what to do.

I looked and looked for a special stocking to buy;
It could not bring you back – but it would be for you.
And so I hung it up along with ours for this Christmas.

I realized that you are truly home and at peace with GOD;
You remain in our hearts as you did leaving home years ago!
But now you have returned in a spiritual way to be with us.

I found a perfect stocking to buy so I could be reminded of you.
A beautiful maroon colored stocking that you loved so much;
It was velvet with gold-tassels edged with many colored sequins.

The sequins are reflecting the light from the tree as from you;
Your spirit fills the room as you did when once you were here;
My heart smiles, I feel you with me once again and you are here!

Others may think the stocking is empty and doesn't belong there;
But not to me – because it is full of you and memories you bring;
You are always cherished and never forgotten and very much loved!

You live on in me and are always within my heart – never to be apart;
This Christmas I have hung your stocking along with ours on the wall;
Your love lives on in us and your love is with us in this empty stocking!

A VEIL OF TEARS

*A have a veil of tears covering my face;
And, yet no one sees my tears but YOU.*

*I feel empty and so broken and alone;
I continue as I push through the pain;*

*I do not know where I am going to go –
With a broken heart only YOU can mend.*

*I peek in a mirror and see how aged I look;
It is strange to see how my face has changed!*

*I wonder if this is what grief feels like inside –
A mask covering me from seeing all I knew.*

*Yet, my faith keeps on telling me deep inside;
YOU will restore me from the ashes in my life!*

*Someday, YOU will take the mask of tears away.
YOU restore me for YOUR Glory to shine in me.*

*While I wait, I go on and trust in YOUR WORD;
That my veil of tears and pain will soon disappear!*

Trusting in

God....

I Am More

Than

I Think I Am

Being More

We were never made to be caterpillars
to crawl around or to be shy;
GOD made us to be butterflies with
beautiful wings so we can fly!

BUTTERFLIES

The beauty of the butterfly always seems to remind me;
That I am more than I would ever think I could even be!!

Because, first they started their life as simple caterpillars!
They crawled around wondering what life was all about!!

How often, when life struggles surround and overwhelm me;
Do I too wonder what my life is all about and if worthwhile??

Do I know that I am bigger than the problems which surround me?
Do I know that I can do many things that I once was afraid to try!

For today I know that I am more than what I thought I could be!
Today, I go through doors of fear with wings I never knew I had.

With these new wings; I know that I can fly as high as I want!
I can tell others that they can fly and reach limits to the sky!!

So we can be more now than we ever thought we could ever be;
And like the butterfly, with beautiful wings, we can soar on high!

We – you and me – were never meant to crawl or to creep around.
We were made to show beauty to the world on wings meant to fly!

Let go – and sprout your wings and open wide so that you can fly.
If you just trust in ME, that I made you beautiful – my butterfly!!

GOD has written to each and every one of us HIS words in the form of HIS Love Letter;
They were written to find HIM there, to read them each day to know and love HIM better!

GOD'S LOVE LETTER

LORD, YOU wrote words for me to live by so I could cope!
YOU inspired great minds of mortal men with YOUR spirit;
They then wrote YOUR Love Letters so I would know hope.

YOU spoke in such a form that YOUR teachings live on today.
YOUR Words remain new and still are able to refresh my soul.
Each day I seek YOU in these letters; I do so I will know the way!

I go to the Word to praise YOU & be comforted by YOU as well;
I have a way to continually find YOU so YOU can speak to me!
All I seek and all I need; I find in YOUR letter where YOU dwell.

YOU said, "Seek ye the kingdom of GOD, and it shall be yours";
I smile with joy and find comfort to know that is YOUR promise;
YOUR Personal Love Letter is the key so that my inner spirit soars!!

*For many of us to sit down to write about our inner
self is very tough!
But once we start it becomes easier to do and one
page is not enough!*

HAVING A JOURNAL

*Writing is the most personal form of prayer for many of us;
We get in touch with inner feelings as we reveal them on paper!
Our longings-fears-strengths-joys and sorrows become exposed!
We are writing to GOD who understands us more than we know!*

*HE constantly showers us with HIS love for us as we dare open up.
When we are confused, we take the pen and write in a form of prayer!
We are patient until we receive our answer from HIM to whom we pray!
WE need a listening heart – it is GOD who is aware and hears our pleas.*

*When we write, we allow the spirit within us to rise above us to release
All of our emotions that are deep within us that we often want to hide!!
When we write we are able to begin to comprehend this thing called life;
Writing allows us to open our hearts on the empty page if we only dare!*

*So often life happens and our experiences need to become our teachers!!
For some reason, we never take the time to learn the lessons from them.
Our "journal" then becomes a "lesson plan" as well as a "prayer book"!
When we write, we open ourselves to GOD's Love and Understanding.*

*We need to trust that GOD understands our very being and our emotions!
HE will never abandon us and instead encourages us to grow to be more!
This "prayer book" – "Journal" is our lesson plan to conquer our struggles;
Heartaches we share lead to discovery; then recovery; and then gratitude!*

*If you only knew that you are writing to Someone who hears all your words;
If you knew, GOD believes in you no matter how you felt – would you write?
It takes courage to take that first step to pick up your pen and begin to write!!
Believe as I had to learn; writing more and more, HE will draw closer to you!*

I am never alone unless I choose to shut myself off in my inner shell;
But If I open up to GOD I will never be trapped in my own prison cell.

<u>HELP ME TO OPEN UP</u>

Lord, help me to open up to YOU;
My inner shell is so tightly closed!

I want to open up completely to YOU;
I want to believe in all YOUR Promises!

I want to believe in YOUR Love just for me;
I know that I am precious in YOUR Sight!

I am a bright shining star in YOUR Universe;
I am YOUR Beloved Child whom YOU love!

And, I am one whom YOU are so pleased with;
YOU hold me in the Palm of YOUR Hand!

YOUR love is so hard for me to understand;
Because I always thought I had to be perfect...

Perfect so that YOU would always love me; but –
I just have to open up and to simply be myself!

Just as YOU made me to be the person I am;
I am Your Greatest Creation in all the world!

The greatest Miracle that YOU ever made – ME!

I have often read in the Bible that my GOD is
described as "I am who am";
We find it easy to see HIS wonder in the rose
and maybe that was HIS plan!

I AM THAT AM

I look at the rose and I always wonder at its beauty;
Yet there is so much of life that I do not understand.
My view of the world is often so very small in its view;
But, in the beauty of the rose I get to know YOU more!

I have discovered YOU in the moment that is "now"!
YOU do not live in "yesterday" nor live in "tomorrow"!
YOU are here and YOU can only be found in the "now"!
YOU are the GOD who lives in the "Present Moment"!

I have found you within the essence of my inner soul!
Like the rose, I must open my heart up to YOU to know!
To find the way to learn, "I am in YOU – YOU are in me"!
This can only be done when I live in the "Present Moment"!

YOU are not the GOD that "was" for I cannot find YOU there!
YOU are not the GOD that "will be" for I cannot leap over there!
YOU are the GOD "who is" and that is the only way to find YOU!
I must seek YOU here and now, if I am to find "I AM THAT AM"!

Leaning on God I will always become very strong!
Leaning on self is when I can and will go wrong!

I AM WEAK - YOU ARE STRONG

I am weak....but, YOU are very strong.
Like the tornado or the mountains are;
Or the fiercest winds and strongest stone;
They represent strength to each one of us;
But, in YOU I need to find my strength;
So that I can be all YOU created me to be!
I reach out – YOU draw me to YOUR Heart...,
I become complete where once was empty space;
I am weak....but, with YOU I am always strong.

Trusting in myself I will surely die – but trusting
in GOD I can fly...
And, when I trust in GOD, I can reach out and
touch the sky!

I CAN FLY

I love to watch the birds as they fly up into the air;
Up they go; how I wish I could fly but I do not dare!
The joy it must be to fly and soar so high and far to see!
Why must I remain grounded; not to fly and not be free?
I want to fly but I am held by gravity that I want to test!
I think about the baby bird that sits so safely in its nest;
Then momma bird decides it's time for baby to try to fly,
She pushes baby out from the safe nest in the tree so high.

The baby squawks and screams while it is falling into space;
And, with a bang, this tiny baby lands so hard it loses its grace!
Shocked and scared, the baby must wonder what this was about.
Momma squawks at baby knowing that it must rid itself of doubt!
Nature has its rules for baby to survive, so baby must continue to try.
While baby wants to stop so it can return to the nest where it was dry!
Baby wonders at what seems insane – not realizing momma knows best.
So, in spite of bumps and bruises, momma wants baby to fly from the nest.

Baby then finds by spreading its wings that it is flying and does not fall;
What a crazy way for a baby bird to learn how to fly when it is so small!
Yet, seeing this, I wonder if this must be the way for us to learn as well...,
We stumble and we fall, and then we ask what this is all about as we yell;
What finally tells us this lesson is hard but it is how we learn who we are?
Like the baby bird, we get our bumps and bruises before we reach our star!
Before reaching our goal, we want to stop from fear to refuse to try any more;
Fortunately, something arises within us, if we allow it to, so that we can soar!!

Can you believe it is GOD who knows and tells us that HE has more in life for us?
HE knows we fall; but if we get up, we are like the bird who tried so HE can bless!
Bless us to reach our visions and become the person that GOD knows we truly are.
But, when we hold back and stop trying, our visions then are blocked and seem so far!
GOD Loves us so much and asks us to be more than we think we are if we but only try;
So that we can learn that life's bumps and bruises teach us to believe that we can fly!
For this, we need to realize GOD wants abundance for us and for us to reach the sky!
We must place our trust in HIM to teach us to fly, not to stay in the nest just to die!!

*Meditation is the stillness within me and not the time
to deal with concern;
It is when I seek the LORD to listen for HIS voice
speaking for me to learn!*

<u>IN THE STILLNESS</u>

*As I meditate, I go within where the stillness waits for me;
My mind is still and still I wait but so often I find it difficult!*

*But, I need to wait in the stillness of these special moments;
Often my mind struggles because I want to fill it with things!*

*YOU have told us many times, "Be still and know I am GOD";
To empty my mind of everything else so I can hear YOUR voice!*

*Emptiness scares us so because we are all so afraid of that place;
Where if that is all there is; it means we are alone with only self!*

*But, with discipline and struggle we can be in a moment of silence;
And find it can bring with it much serenity and a feeling of peace!*

*Stillness – this emptiness of ourself allows room for YOU in there;
Because during precious times of stillness I am saying yes to YOU!*

*YOU have promised and said to us, "I am in you and you are in ME!"
Yet, how often we feel separated or far and very much apart from YOU?*

*Why is that? Surely, it is because we do not dare to enter the stillness!
For it is only in the stillness that we encounter the truth of what we seek!*

*Too often I seek outside for YOU or for peace when it is there within!
Within, I find YOU and peace that can only be found while being still.*

*I offer up all I am to YOU and in this solemn, quiet moment of silence;
I hear YOU say, "I give you all of ME and all MY Love" in the stillness!*

My soul dances with joy as I open my music box
and it plays its song;
Its melody touches my soul and I am filled with
such joy all day long!

MY MUSIC BOX

How I love to turn and wind my music box as I crank, crank and crank;
A chafing sound, but it is necessary to make before my music box will play!
There it is – its song – the sound of notes blending high notes and low notes;
It plays such a melody so rich that it reaches in and draws my soul to hear!
The house fills with joy as the song plays on and on playing a tune I so enjoy!
Each of its notes is lifting my Spirit higher to a lofty place of such comfort!
Life is like that music box because we must crank, crank and crank ourselves;
To get in tune with YOU. High notes are easy to attain, at happy, joyful times!
The low ones come through in the form of our sorrow, pain, & troubled days.
Yet, we need to experience both, in order for our life to play a beautiful song;
If all we had were high notes alone; we would have only screaming sounds;
While if all we had were low notes alone; they would cause a groaning sound!
Joined together, our life blends as the sounds mix and create beautiful songs!
Music brings the essence of my soul out – making me feel alive and connected;
Music goes beyond all outward appearances to enter the very core of my soul!
My soul responds as music brings me back to YOU and the awareness that…
I am always one with YOU and YOU with me, no matter the circumstances!
I am whole once more and my soul responds – so play on, my little music box!

Looking up at the galaxies in the heavens at night has led me to ask;
If holding all of life and all the wonder of the stars is a very big task?

THE WONDER OF THE STARS

I stand outside on a very dark night;
Looking up at a beautiful bright sky!
I see stars sending their shining light;
Stars perfectly placed and I ask why!

How can there be this order in the sky?
Each star seems to know its place is true;
This order that often leads me to ask why;
Who holds the plan to this glorious view?

I stand wondering as these stars shine;
When so often I feel insecure and alone!
You made these stars for me as a sign;
To look for YOU & see the unknown!

You hold each and every star in place;
And, gently YOU remind me just in case;
I forget – it is YOU who gives me grace!
To let me see I am in the right space!

YOU see the beauty and wonder of me;
Like the stars that shine ever so bright!
YOU call me to shine for others to see;
Not as stars in the sky but near in sight.

I can lighten the way for the weary soul;
Bring them the warmth of YOUR Light!
Warmth YOU have given me in my soul;
To let others be stars for YOU as bright!

Am I really more than I think I can be?
YOUR Love lives in me every single day.
You ask me to be a star so others can see;
By my light I help to show them the way.

You have placed me where YOU want me;
I put my trust in YOU and in YOUR plan!
I know perfect order is so that we can see;
That YOU Loved us ever since time began!

When I start to question my life or my place;
I know YOU have a plan for me to pursue;
If times are tough and more than I can face;
YOUR Love & answers will get me through!

When I am confused I need to look to recall;
To realize YOU were with me before I began!
And look in the sky to see the wonder of it all;
The wonder of the stars & me in YOUR plan!

How is it that I can see the beauty of God's creation
in all things around me?
But the most precious gift HE has ever made is me
which I have failed to see!

THE WONDER OF YOU

My children – I Love you beyond all your limited understanding;
For you are the creation of MY Heart filled with all my Love!
And, of all that is in MY creation, I chose only to dwell within you;
You are MY children who can see beyond the beauty around you!

You see MY Hand which is in the majesty of the tall mountains;
You see MY hand that is in the roar of the mighty waves of the sea;
You see MY Hand living in the different colors of beautiful flowers;
You see MY Hand in the various animals, butterflies and all the birds!

You see MY Hand in the universe whose splendor is made just for you;
You see the moon and see the stars in the heavens so vast to your eyes;
All of this beauty and all these wonders were made for you to behold;
Yet, how is it that you fail to see the best I made – the wonder of you?

Look within the mirror "MY Children" to see MY "greatest miracle"!
You alone are MY greatest creation for there is no one else like you!
I called you by name and you are the most precious beauty in MY eyes;
For it is only in YOU that I can live to have a very personal relationship!

It is only in you that MY Spirit dwells to live and love so many others;
I am in your heart, arms and legs for me to bless another through you!
Never forget who you are; so look in the mirror to see what I have made!
Look to see into your own eyes so you can see that they shine with ME!

Rejoice in all I have created for you and rejoice in who you really are;
I have made no mistakes and so you know you are my greatest miracle!
So if you have not seen it before, begin to see the gift I have given is you!
You are precious in my eyes and know that I rejoice in the wonder of you!

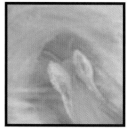

If you are like me, you may want to change to be
transformed into something new!
The reality is, when we search for God's Light, we
find it already inside me and you!

Painting by Barbara Jacobbe

<u>TRANSFORMED</u>

I seek the light not knowing the Light is seeking me;
When the darkness of this world is surrounding me!
I become less than I am since I am feeling so afraid;
Then my GOD comes to me in so many different ways!

HE gently whispers to me, "MY child, you are MINE"!
"You are full of MY Light and there is nothing to fear"!
"You are safe with me and I will hold you in MY arms"!
"YOU have forgotten who you are; MY daughter of Light"!

When I listen is when I allow HIS Light to transform me;
I feel the warmth of HIS Love surround my inner being!
I breathe in HIS peace and healing into my whole body;
It is during this time that I remember how precious I am!

There is nothing else I need to do when I stay in HIS Light;
I just need to have the desire to be one with the Light of GOD!
It is then that all things are possible for me to do in HIS Power;
I am HIS child and transformed – to be more than I dared to be!

Each of us is surrounded by such glowing love
that we can always give to others!
The Love of GOD is shining through our Halo
making us all sisters and brothers!

YOUR HALO

Is your halo on, and if it is, is it crooked or is it straight?
However it is on is not what makes you either rich or great!
It is your Halo that shows the Light that shines from you;
And what is deep inside you that reflects the good you do!

Your Halo is GOD'S gift that reflects the Love you give to others from within!
That love brings you life as well as everyone else whether they be friend or kin!
The more love you give of you; the more your Halo shines like a precious gem!
GOD cannot contain Himself for it is through you HE brings HIS Love to them!

HE shines through you every day; but you need to let HIM be shown to begin;
Begin showing Him to others through you; that is how I know GOD really has skin!
HE uses you to reach out to others whose spirits are down and they are so broken;
This is how our Loving GOD works that he delivers all the Promises HE has spoken!

Who else but you can show someone else the way so they can rise and also shine?
When they are broken and so lost – you can show your love to listen and be kind!
You can listen with a heart which does not condemn or make others to feel small;
Who else but you is able to help someone to get right up after they trip or they fall?

Who else but you can bring Light into a sullen world darkened by storm and rain;
Where people are burdened by so many problems in life that they are full of pain?
Who else but you can show someone Love when you listen, understand and care;
Especially when they feel beaten down to the point beyond which they can not bear?

GOD in HIS Divine Plan created each of us to serve those we encounter and meet;
We see them on the road of life where we can help them get up and stay on their feet!
We can help them bear their burdens and heartaches when we help them dry a tear;
This is because we are called to bring HIS Love wherever we can to those far or near!

So shine your Light whenever and let your Halo be seen even if you think it is small;
The more you let your Light shine out the more it will help someone from taking a fall!
Give what you have to every person you meet and your Halo can only grow and grow;
This Halo of Light will spark those needing it in the world & the flame of Love will glow!

You Are A

Winner

In *God's* Eyes

The Ocean of

God's Abundance

No one knows how powerful and peaceful one very small light can be.
Until you put a thousand candles all lit together for everyone to see!

LIGHT IN THE DARKNESS

The darkness can be overwhelming like news we find in the world!

Wars that seem to never end with children wounded and starving;

So many unkind actions…I feel so powerless when I cannot help!

Staying in denial…helps one to cope…but YOU call us to reach out;

Even when we are not able to do much; everyone can do something!

A simple act of kindness is how I can do small things with great love!

YOUR Love lives within us so we can Love those You call for us to love!

Sometimes we do not know how or where we find the light in the darkness!

The light lives within me – within us, for YOU are there, calling us to shine!

What I think is my little light, can shine like a small candle in the darkness.

If all of us decided to light our candle…no matter how small we think it is;

The darkness could disappear just from the brilliance of so many little lights!

We brighten the world with acts of kindness to bring "Light in the darkness"!

*One will never consider themself as a victor if the
thought is not ever in their heart;
The truth is we will never be a winner if we don't
believe we are one or we never start!*

YOU ARE A WINNER

Who has won __FIRST PLACE__ in GOD's loving heart?	*You!!*
Who has won __FIRST PLACE__ from the very first start?	*You!!*
Who has won __FIRST PLACE__ worth more than gold?	*You!!*
Who has won __FIRST PLACE__ as a wonder to behold?	*You!!*
Who has won __FIRST PLACE__ to be always cherished?	*You!!*
Who has won __FIRST PLACE__ promised not to perish?	*You!!*
Who has won __FIRST PLACE__ in your friend's eyes?	*You!!*
Who has won __FIRST PLACE__ as bright as the stars?	*You!!*
Who has won __FIRST PLACE__ for beauty as the flower?	*You!!*
Who has won __FIRST PLACE__ as the queen of the hour!	*You!!*
Who has won __FIRST PLACE__ showing others you cared?	*You!!*
Who has won __FIRST PLACE__ to be more than you dared?	*You!!*

*God created you to always be a winner in everything no matter where!
Learn you are more than you ever could imagine or even think or dare!
So accept your trophy & medal and live a winner forever as GOD's heir!*

We all have dreamed that we could be queen for just a day!
Become all that you are and the dream will never go away!

IT IS GOOD TO BE QUEEN

You are always a woman of dignity and honor;
For you were created special by a Loving God!
To claim your title that you are forever precious;
You must believe you are Queen in God's eyes!
Jewels of love, kindness, abundance adorn you!
The crown you wear is full of many brilliant stars!
Splendor and wonder are the long robes you wear;
They are made of dazzling gold not heavy but light!
They will keep you safe so no danger can harm you!
You are far more than you ever realized or believed!
Perhaps this is because no one has ever told you this:
"The queen and jewel of a Loving GOD is who you are"!
"The day you were born…a bright star shone in Heaven";
"Angels rejoiced and sang hearing your beautiful name"!
"The throne of a queen awaits you - but you must claim it"!
"Believe in yourself and who you are and your crown awaits"!
"You deserve love & to be loved; treated with dignity and honor"!
"Remove all negative energy - you deserve circles of positive energy";
"If negative energy enters, shout, "Be gone, I will have none of this""!
"Claim your throne so that you can be all God has created you to be";
"And, put the crown of all possibilities upon your head for all to see".
"Reign forever in glory, love and peace…IT IS GOOD TO BE QUEEN"!

Order Form

Item

Book: "Trusting In God.....I Am More Than I Think I Am"

Qty: _____ @ $19.95 = _____

   MA Residents add 5% Tax: _____

   Shipping @ 1.95 for 1 book _____

     @ 1.75 (2-3)

     @ 1.50 (4 or more)

      Order Total: $ _____

Ship To:

Name: _____

Street: _____

City-State: _____

Zip: _____

Method of Payment

_____ **Check Enclosed**

_____ **Credit Card**

_____ **M//C** _____ **Visa**

_____ Card #

_____ Exp. Date

sign_____
Signature

Note: Allow 7-10 business days for delivery.

"Inward Reflections" ^{TM}

® pending

Mail Order To:

Inward Reflections, Inc.

P. O. Box 1747

Brockton, MA 02302

<u>Order Form</u>

<u>Item</u>

<u>Book:</u> "Trusting In God.....I Am More Than I Think I Am"

<u>Qty:</u> _____ @ $19.95 = _____

MA Residents add 5% Tax: _____

Shipping @ 1.95 for 1 book _____

@ 1.75 (2-3)

@ 1.50 (4 or more)

<u>Order Total:</u> $ _____

<u>Ship To:</u>

<u>Name:</u> _____

<u>Street:</u> _____

<u>City-State</u>: _____

<u>Zip</u>: _____

<u>Method of Payment</u>

_____ **Check Enclosed**

_____ **Credit Card**

_____ **M//C** _____ **Visa**

_____ Card #

_____ Exp. Date

sign_____
Signature

Note: Allow 7-10 business days for delivery.

"Inward Reflections" ™

® pending

Mail Order To:

Inward Reflections, Inc.

P. O. Box 1747

Brockton, MA 02302